Rhode
Island
CURIOSITIES

Help Us Keep This Guide Up to Date

Every effort has been made by the author and editors to make this guide as accurate and useful as possible. However, many things can change after a guide is published—establishments close, phone numbers change, hiking trails are rerouted, facilities come under new management, etc.

We would love to hear from you concerning your experiences with this guide and how you feel it could be made better and be kept up to date. While we may not be able to respond to all comments and suggestions, we'll take them to heart and we'll also make certain to share them with the author. Please send your comments and suggestions to the following address:

The Globe Pequot Press
Reader Response/Editorial Department
P.O. Box 480
Guilford, CT 06437

Or you may e-mail us at:

editorial@GlobePequot.com

Thanks for your input, and happy travels!

Rhode Island
CURIOSITIES

QUIRKY CHARACTERS, ROADSIDE ODDITIES & OTHER OFFBEAT STUFF

SETH BROWN

INSIDERS' GUIDE®

GUILFORD, CONNECTICUT

AN IMPRINT OF THE GLOBE PEQUOT PRESS

To buy books in quantity for corporate use or incentives, call **(800) 962–0973** or e-mail **premiums@GlobePequot.com**.

INSIDERS' GUIDE®

Copyright © 2007 by Morris Book Publishing, LLC

Text design by Nancy Freeborn
Layout by Debbie Nicolais
Maps by Rusty Nelson © Morris Book Publishing, LLC
Photo credits: p. 45 Richard Kizirian; p. 57 Michaela Andrews; p. 103 Paul G. DuHamel; p. 105 Cryil Place; p. 177 Thomas Noel; p. 259 Bryan Lucas/The Chorus of Westerly; p. 280 Courtesy of Matt The Knife. All other photos are by the author.

Library of Congress Cataloging-in-Publication Data is available.
ISBN: 978-0-7627-4338-4

Manufactured in the United States of America
First Edition/First Printing

To my family:

Not only one of the more curious things in Rhode Island, but also my favorite.

RHODE ISLAND

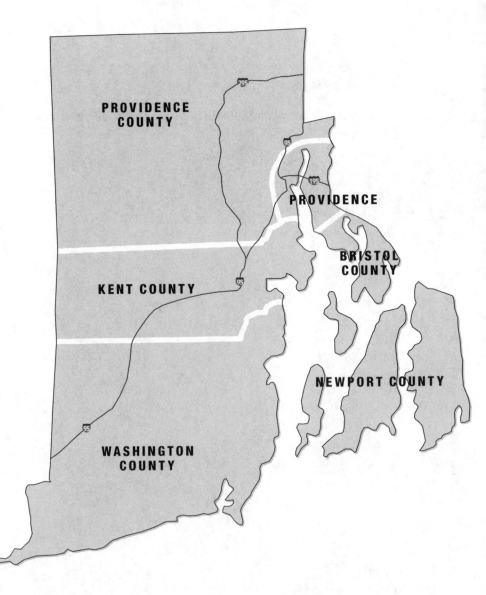

Contents

Acknowledgments

First and foremost, I have to thank everyone who took the time to answer my questions and talk with me. Some of the people in this book were in the middle of touring the world, and made the time to tell me a little about themselves before rushing off to Thailand (Len) or while recovering from China (Matt). Some of the people even went beyond the call of duty to make sure I could interview them, and managed to find me when I had failed to find them (thanks, Scott). The book, without the cooperation of these people, would just be a collection of buildings, so I thank them heartily for their assistance.

East Greenwich librarian Diane Hogan was also very helpful in providing information, in spite of the fact that she was not going to be appearing in the main part of the book, so I owe her at least this sentence for reminding me why I love libraries and librarians.

Naturally, I must thank my editor, Gillian Belnap, both for encouraging me through the writing process and for being understanding when I revealed to her that I was not a cartographer.

My friends, as always, were very supportive during this entire process and helped me maintain my sanity as deadlines closed—or, at least as much as I started with. Spleen weasel.

Finally, I must thank my family. Not just because everyone thanks their family on the acknowledgments page, but because this book really ended up being a family experience. My family is Rhode Island to me, since I was born and raised in the company of both. My father was also born and raised in Rhode Island, and his vast knowledge of the state was an invaluable asset when writing this book. But more than that, writing this book served as an excuse to explore the state we love, together.

Sometimes with my father, sometimes with my mother, sometimes with my sister, occasionally even with my brother, we drove all over the state and saw interesting places and met interesting people. I'm not sure I could have done it without them, but I am sure that I would not have enjoyed it nearly as much.

Thanks.

Introduction

I love Rhode Island.

That's the short version. The rest of this book is the long version, but Rhode Island is the state I love, and who I am. Yes, it's true that I ended up moving to Massachusetts a few years ago, but I'm a Rhode Islander. I don't jump when I hear "Massachusetts" on the news, but I listen to any story about Rhode Island with piqued interest. Meeting someone else from Massachusetts while traveling is pleasant, but if I meet someone from Rhode Island, I get excited and start asking who they know.

None of this is to knock Massachusetts. It's a fine state, but it's not Rhode Island. Rhode Island is home. Sometimes, when I'd start writing profiles on things I remember from my childhood, I'd get lost in nostalgia. I remember images, feelings of excitement. And Rhode Island is still home to me—always will be. Whenever the car I'm in crosses into Rhode Island while on a long trip, I reflexively raise my arms in triumph. I'm almost shedding a tear writing this, and I'm not a man given to excess emotion.

Why does Rhode Island inspire this unique kind of loyalty? Well, it's small. Small enough that everyone knows everyone, because the whole state feels like a big town. In a sense it is, because everyone lives roughly as close to each other as they would in a town in some big state. That's the advantage of a small state; we're all just a short drive away from Providence.

Believe me, that fact made writing this book a whole lot easier. If you're going to go back and forth across a state fifty times to research a book, Rhode Island is the best one to pick. (I'm sure glad I didn't grow up in Texas.) This will also come in handy for you if you decide to go visiting some of the locations in this book. They're all a short drive from each other. And heck, you could take a day to walk through downtown Providence and catch a dozen of them.

Did I mention Rhode Island was small? We divide it into five counties, but there is no county government. There are more than three dozen municipalities with their own local government. There are also neighborhoods and villages within the municipalities, and a wonderful array of Indian names that give you an idea of Rhode Island's history. Narragansett, Pawtucket, Chepachet, Quonset, Apponaug, Misquamicut . . . hard to spell, but fun to say. And our language isn't just Indian. We drink "cabinets" and eat "gaggers," called "milk shakes" and "hot dogs" by the rest of the less civilized world.

Rhode Island is full of treasures. We have the first Baptist church in America, and the first street in the country to use gaslights. And yes, we have the quahog, though there's no town named that in spite of what *Family Guy* may have led you to believe. Some of the more well-known treasures have been left out of this book, because you already know about them. Then again, it would be impossible for me to write a book about Rhode Island and not include certain things like the Big Blue Bug, even though everyone already knows about it.

Still, many of the people and places in this book should be new to you. There's a workshop filled with bizarre giant living puppets, just down the street from a disappearing diner. There's Chinese food with a side of either jazz or Jews, depending on your preference. There are people who build rock sculptures and eat bugs. And if you live in Rhode Island, they're all just a short drive away.

So what are you waiting for? Start reading, and get going!

PROVIDENCE

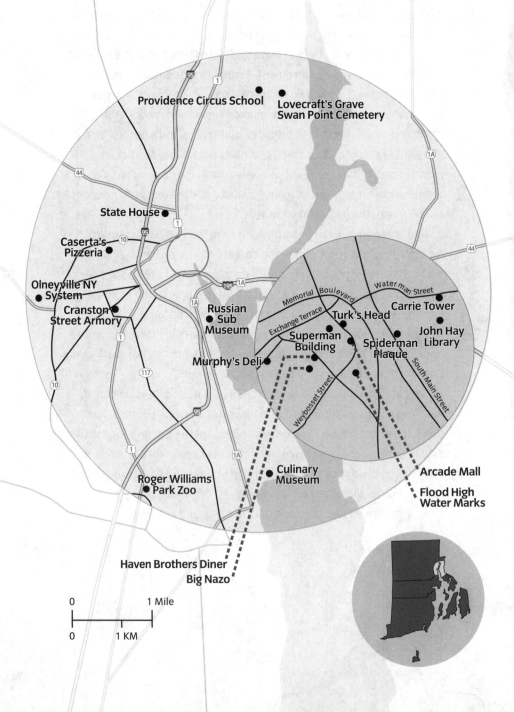

Providence Circus School

Lovecraft's Grave
Swan Point Cemetery

State House

Caserta's
Pizzeria

Olneyville NY
System

Cranston
Street Armory

Russian
Sub
Museum

Murphy's Deli

Memorial Boulevard

Waterman Street

Exchange Terrace

Turk's Head

Carrie Tower

Superman
Building

Spiderman
Plaque

John Hay
Library

South Main Street

Weybosset Street

Culinary
Museum

Arcade Mall

Flood High
Water Marks

Roger Williams
Park Zoo

Haven Brothers Diner

Big Nazo

0   1 Mile

0   1 KM

PROVIDENCE

Wiener Takes All

Nothing says Rhode Island quite like New York—New York System, that is. In spite of the name, New York System wieners are only available in Rhode Island. While not exactly haute cuisine, Rhode Islanders often find themselves hungering for a few delectable wieners from this glorious grease-ridden institution. New York System wiener shops are all over Rhode Island, open late, and generally provide food for a buck.

Now, the first thing to note about wieners is that they are not hot dogs. Some people will tell you that "wiener" is just another name for "hot dog," but these are the same folks who try to tell you that "Chanukah" is just another name for "Christmas." Hot dogs are made from beef and tied off at the end. Not that there's anything wrong with that, but wieners are a different beast entirely. A wiener is made of pork, and sometimes veal. And instead of having each wiener tied off, they are simply cut on the ends. While they are definitely not hot dogs, they have acquired other nicknames, such as bellybuster and gagger (pronounced *bellybustah* and *gaggah* by native Rhode Islanders).

New York System began back in 1927 when Gust Pappas came over from Greece. He had a little wiener cart and decided to name it "New York System" to honor New York City, having come through Ellis Island when he had migrated. The cart eventually became a shop on 424 Smith Street, which has stayed in the Pappas family for three generations, passing through Gust's son, Ernie, and now resting in the hands of Ernie's son, Gus. In addition to ownership of the wiener shop, Gus Pappas has inherited the Secret Recipe for New York System meat sauce, which is what truly makes a NY System wiener what it is. Not even the other employees at New York System know the secret ingredients in the spice.

Every time I look at this photo, I get hungry.

These days there are New York System wiener shops all over Rhode Island, but not owned by Pappas. Apparently Ernie Pappas's brother, cousin, uncle, and former neighbor each opened their own New York System shop, and borrowed the recipe. (Now you know why Gus Pappas keeps the recipe a secret.) But wherever you go to get your hot wieners, you should know what to expect: a hot pork wiener in a steamed bun, slathered with meat sauce and mustard, and sprinkled with onions and celery salt. This is the important list of wiener toppings, and ordered by demanding your wieners "all the way." They generally cost somewhere around a buck apiece, though only a novice would order a single hot wiener. They should be ordered three or more at a time, so the shopkeeper can line up the wieners on his arm and sauce them all in a row.

> *What's the best deal on lunch in the state?*
> *It's New York System wieners; they're great!*
> *Wednesday lunch, have a few,*
> *And you'll taste them at two,*
> *And once more Thursday morning at eight.*

Despite the fact that the Smith Street shop was the first, today the most popular spot for New York System wieners is probably the Olneyville, East Providence, location at 20 Plainfield Street (401–621–9500; www.olneyvillenysystem.com). They've been serving wieners since 1946, and perhaps most importantly, they're open until 2:00 A.M. every day of the week for your late-night wiener cravings.

Not Just Club Soda

Ever wonder what the heck *club soda* means?

Do they mean that it's a triple-decker soda?

Or perhaps that you should take a bottle of soda and beat someone over the head with it?

I wouldn't drink something with a name like that, especially from a big multinational corporation that makes nebulous drinks. Nosireebob, I'd rather drink a soda made in Rhode Island for nearly a century—Yacht Club Soda. That's the name of the company, not the flavor of the soda. And they tell you what kind of club it is right up front: a yacht club.

In addition to avoiding ambiguity, Yacht Club Soda has been a Rhode Island production since 1915, microbrewing their own old-fashioned soda in delicious flavors like sarsaparilla and birch beer. And the recipes have stayed the same ever since then. The owner, William Sgambato, won't reveal what those recipes are. Fair enough. But what he will say is that just like when they first started making soda, the main ingredients are artesian well water and cane sugar. And if you ask real nicely, he'll mention things like vanilla extract in the cream soda. He would know—he tastes each batch himself, to make sure the flavor is right.

The Sgambatos have been working at Yacht Club Soda since 1935, when Bill was a young boy of thirteen. But it wasn't until 1961 that Bill and his father bought the company. Bill's sons, Mike and John, took over running the company a few years ago, and they continue to make the microbrewed soda in the same traditional way.

PROVIDENCE

Aside from the fact that they use superior ingredients, that's about all you're likely to learn about their recipes. Other upstart soda companies pop out of nowhere and claim to make old-fashioned soda, so the Sgambatos knows that their actual old-fashioned recipe needs to be kept safe, although most of the big manufacturers couldn't make it anyway. Hand-brewing soda takes time, using cane sugar instead of high-fructose corn syrup takes money, most soda companies don't have the benefit of an artesian well to provide pure water, and no multinational corporation would have the patience for the relatively slow speeds of the old machinery at the Yacht Club Bottling Works.

How old is the machinery? Well, the newest machine is the bottle washer, and that was made in 1948. Yes, they need a bottle washer, because they still use glass bottles.

The heyday of Yacht Club Soda was more than half a century ago, but recently they have made a push to start distributing once again. Although their North Providence factory floor may be no larger than an apartment, the taste of Yacht Club Soda is known throughout Rhode Island. Anyone who has lived in the state for a couple decades likely has fond memories of the sweet and lightly carbonated soda.

And while only Rhode Islanders might have heard of Yacht Club Soda ten or twenty years ago, they are making a resurgence. In addition to distributing to other states, they are increasing local distribution and maintain a healthy presence at various Rhode Island events.

To find out where they'll be next, check the events section of their Web site at www.yachtclubsoda.com.

WHEN IN ROME . . .

There are those who have charged that Rhode Island is too small to be a state. But we all know that people obsessed with size are usually making up for some of their own shortcomings. Still, there is something to be said for the idea that Rhode Island could function as a city-state. After all, in terms of common bond, Rhode Island does function like a city-state. When traveling far from the East Coast, meeting someone else from Rhode Island is much more exciting than simply meeting someone else from your home state. It's really more like meeting someone else from your own city. And unlike most states (and like most cities), if two Rhode Islanders should chance to cross paths while abroad, they will talk about who they know until they find a common acquaintance. For longtime Rhode Islanders, there is always a common acquaintance.

Ancient Rome was probably the world's most famous city-state, and Rhode Island has many similarities. Rome was built on seven hills. Providence was also built on seven hills: Constitution, College, Christian, Smith, Tockwotten, Weybosset, and Federal. In fact, Federal Hill is the district known as "Little Italy," with almost as much Italian culture as Rome itself. Some might even argue that Federal Hill has better Italian food.

Providence may well be the new Rome. And to most people not from the East Coast, Rhode Island may as well be Providence. If you're describing where you live to a West Coaster, "near Providence" is probably fine. When I mean Buddy Cianci was in charge of Providence, everyone knew the mayor. Many people, however, did not know who the governor was. But it wasn't important. Providence was our city-state, and even if you didn't technically live there, you did. You know what they say: "All roads lead to Providence."

PROVIDENCE

Arcane Arcade

If you said you were going to the arcade, some kids today are so used to having video games in their living room that they wouldn't know what you mean. But if I said I was going to the Arcade to go shopping, you might not know what I was talking about. Who's the whippersnapper now? Well, before they became associated with video games, arcades were big roof-covered lanes with shops on both sides. And before that, an arcade just meant a series of arches supported by columns and pillars. Both of the older meanings apply to the Providence Arcade, which is the oldest indoor shopping mall in America.

The Arcade was built long ago, in 1828, back when Providence was a prosperous seaport. Construction of the Arcade was a grand project, requiring the cooperation of two architects: Russell Warren and James Bucklin. Actually, *cooperation* may be a strong word: Each man had his own ideas about how the entrance of the Arcade should look. The solution? Simple: Have two entrances! The Arcade can be entered from Weybosset Street, where the entrance is topped by a parapet, or from Westminster Street, where a pediment sits atop the entrance.

Either way, the entrances to the 216-foot-tall building are impressive. Perhaps their most notable feature are the half-dozen granite columns that support them, each more than 20 feet tall and weighing thirteen tons. It took teams of oxen to drag the columns from the local quarry in Johnston, and in 1828 they were the biggest monoliths in the country. Obviously this is not the case today, but they still shouldn't be taken for granite—even though they are. In fact, the whole building was originally constructed of granite, at a cost of $145,000 (which would be well over $2 million today).

On the downside, once the building was complete, Providence only had 14,000 residents to shop there. On the upside, however, there was very little competition, because not only was it the country's first indoor shopping mall, but it was the first Rhode Island commercial venture of any type established on the west side of the Providence River. More competition has since popped up, but the Arcade remains due to its charm. The architects (especially Warren) created a Greek temple–style building that continues to impress even today. The inside, while it can't compare to the exterior, still features three floors of shops, as well as a large glass skylight across the entire building supported by wooden beams. The upper-floor shops are all connected by long bridges overlooking the bottom floor, and while an elevator has been added to make the building more accessible, the initial charm remains.

The Arcade Mall, fronted by six of those whatever-you-column.

PROVIDENCE

In fact, the Metropolitan Museum of Art once named the Providence Arcade one of the finest commercial buildings in the history of American architecture. What's more, the Arcade has been designated a National Historic Landmark—and a good thing, too, because it almost wasn't around at all. It got very run down over the years, to the point where it was almost demolished in 1944. Thankfully, it was not. The Arcade survived near demolition, as well as a fire, three hurricanes, and a lousy economy. Finally, it was refurbished in 1980 at a cost of nearly $3 million, and its place as a Providence landmark was cemented. The country's oldest indoor mall in a building framed by Greek columns that look even older—it's a little ionic.

You can visit the Arcade—just be sure to bring more than a few quarters. It's at 65 Weybosset Street in downtown Providence. And if for some reason you feel the need to call about the mall, you can reach them at (401) 598–1199.

Cranston Street Castle

The Cranston Street Armory isn't in Cranston, it's in Providence. Just so
we clear that up right away. Anyway, the Cranston Street Armory is a
gigantic building that looms impressively over the west end of Providence, like a castle that got caught in a time warp. And essentially it is
a castle in a time warp, because it managed to go from armory to inauguration hall to Hollywood soundstage all within a century.

The Cranston Street Armory was built in 1907 to house the Rhode
Island National Guard, and it is really, really big—165,000 square feet of
space, to be exact, including a grand central hall as wide as two football fields and as high as fifteen football players stacked head-to-toe on
top of each other. The space wasn't used for football, though, but by a
different set of angry men in uniform grunting a lot while preparing to
do battle. However, the National Guard only needed to drill one day a
week, so with a building so big, they had plenty of people taking different nights. After World War I, the 243rd Coast Artillery began drilling in
the building, and would later be joined by various parts of the 43rd and
118th as well.

Even as far as drill halls go, it was big. It has been said that you could
fit the entire population of Rhode Island inside the Cranston Street
Armory—and really, given the trussed steel roof and the balconies and
skylights, it might not be so bad. The outside of the building is equally
impressive, since the drill hall is flanked on both sides by office blocks
that each have a six-story tower. As you might expect with a building
like that, the rest of Providence's West End was largely built around it—
not only physically, but sometimes socially as well. The Cranston Street
Armory has been called "a castle for the people," because its sheer size
meant it played host to a lot of state functions. During the twentieth
century you could find almost everything happening there, including
track meets, dog shows, charity balls, political balls, political circuses,

and actual circuses. That's the advantage of having a National Guard that only drills once a week.

Unfortunately, rising maintenance and operating costs forced the National Guard to leave the Armory in 1996, and residents feared that this historical building would be lost and destroyed once vacated. Although the castlelike structure is listed on the National Register of Historic Places, was one of the National Trust's Eleven Most Endangered Places for 1997, and has been on the Providence Preservation Society's Top Ten Most Endangered list for a number of years, its fate was uncertain. It was then used by filmmaker Michael Corrente for his film *Outside Providence* in 1997, which sparked hopes that it could become a permanent soundstage.

Sadly, that plan was voted down in the late 1990s, as was a plan to make it the permanent home of the State Archives. A $15.3 million state bond was proposed in 2004 to pay for renovations, but this too was unsuccessful. Finally, in 2006, the Armory building was leased to Disney to shoot their film *Underdog*. And in preparation for this lease, some much-needed maintenance was finally done. But what will be the future of this grand castle, once drill hall, now soundstage?

Frankly, nobody knows. Perhaps you should check it out yourself and see if you can find out. You'll easily find it on the west end of town at 310 Cranston Street.

In a Single Bound

Faster than a speeding bullet. More powerful than a locomotive. It's a bird. It's a plane. It's . . . rumor.

Yes, the son of Kal-El was almost invincible, aside from his crippling weakness to Kryptonite. But rumor refuses to die, which is what lends an extra air of mystery and importance to the already impressive Superman Building at 50 Kennedy Plaza in downtown Providence. The Superman Building is more properly named the Bank of America Building, which was previously the Fleet Bank Tower, and before that the Industrial Trust Tower. But while banks come and go, Superman is forever, and Providence residents have called this building the Superman Building ever since the 1950s.

The reason? With its art deco design and impressive tower, it bears more than a passing resemblance to the *Daily Planet* Building featured in the 1950s Superman comics and television series. And rumor, that most powerful of forces, had it that the *Daily Planet* Building itself was based on this prodigious part of Providence's skyline.

If you were going to pay homage to a building, this isn't a bad one to pick. It was built in 1927 by Walker & Gillette of New York and George Frederick Hall of Providence as the Industrial Trust Tower. At 26 floors and 428 feet, it was not only the tallest building in Rhode Island, but the tallest in all of New England when it was built. The building is actually divided into a central tower with six wings, and the stepped massing was an imitation of New York's skyscrapers of the same era.

So was it really the basis for the Daily Planet Building that Superman always flew over? Well, probably not. While some people do believe that the Industrial Trust Tower was where Clark Kent really went to work, there are New Yorkers who claim that their Daily News Building was the real inspiration for the Daily Planet. Ohio residents insist that the Ohio Bell Building in Cleveland is the true source, and even St.

It's a bird. It's a plane. It's the Superman building.

Louisans have their own Superman Building. When asked point blank where he got the Daily Planet Building, the cartoonist responsible for the design denied that any one building was the source of his inspiration. So there's no proof whatsoever that Providence's Superman Building was the real deal.

Though no longer the tallest we've found,
As a building, it's still quite renowned.
Daily Planet? Could be,
But all people agree
That to leap it takes more than one bound.

However, it cannot be denied that it does look very, very similar. And for this reason, Rhode Islanders continue to call it the Superman Building, even if it probably wasn't the *Daily Planet*. After all, it still looms over Providence as the state's tallest building. And while the OneTen corporation may soon build a residential tower to surpass the Superman Building in height, it cannot be surpassed in grandeur.

PROVIDENCE

All You Need Is Lovecraft

There is perhaps no Rhode Islander better known outside of Rhode Island and less known in it than the late H. P. Lovecraft. The H. P. stands for Howard Phillips, but it may as well stand for Horror Progenitor, as H. P. Lovecraft has probably influenced modern horror more than anyone else. Everyone in the horror world from Stephen King to Clive Barker cites Lovecraft as one of their big influences. Years ago I met a man all the way from France, and when I told him I was from Rhode Island, the first thing he asked was whether I liked H. P. Lovecraft. Yet in spite of his worldwide fame, if you ask a random Rhode Islander what they think of H. P. Lovecraft, there's a 50 percent chance that their response will be "Who?"

Let me briefly explain, for their (and your) benefit. H. P. Lovecraft was born on August 20, 1890, in Providence, and his childhood provided a lot of background for a horror writer. When H. P. was three years old, his father suffered a nervous breakdown and was put in a sanitarium, where he died. Whether nature or nurture, it seemed to run in the family, for Lovecraft's mother also suffered a nervous breakdown years later, for which she too would be institutionalized until her death. Lovecraft avoided the hospitalization-until-death route by having his own nervous breakdown early, at the age of eighteen. The downside was that this breakdown forced him to leave high school, and he never returned to get his diploma.

Lovecraft more than made up for it. Reading and writing from a young age, his interest in science (as well as strange and macabre fiction) had already bloomed before he reached puberty. He was writing journals of astronomy and the like for his friends, and soon took up writing columns in various local newspapers. He eventually began writing short stories, and briefly married a woman named Sonia Greene. Then she had to be put in a sanitarium. Noticing a pattern? Lovecraft left Sonia in 1926, returning to his beloved Providence after two years in New York (which he called "a Babel of sound and filth").

He would spend the rest of his life in Providence, prolifically communicating with the outside world through letters: Some have estimated that Lovecraft wrote nearly 100,000 letters, far outpacing his writings of fiction. However, it was after his final return to Providence that Lovecraft proceeded to write his most well-known fiction, including "At the Mountains of Madness" and the cult classic "The Call of Cthulhu." Many of his stories took place in the imaginary town of Arkham, which he based on Providence. Lovecraft eventually died of cancer in 1937, and was sadly never quite famous during his lifetime.

However, he has achieved much posthumous fame. In addition to his influence on horror and science fiction writers, his Cthulhu Mythos has inspired millions of people and even spawned many tales based in Lovecraft's world. Such is his posthumous popularity, in fact, that although his name was carved onto the family monument in Providence's Swan Point Cemetery when he died, in 1977 a group of fans bought him his own headstone. On this, they inscribed not only his name and dates of existence in this world, but a powerful statement from one of his many, many personal letters: I AM PROVIDENCE.

There is even an annual commemorative service that has been going on since the fiftieth anniversary of his death in 1987. Every year, fans gather to read a eulogy describing Lovecraft's life, a poem by a Providence native called "At Lovecraft's Grave," and all kinds of other things Lovecraft written or themed. Some say that the spirit of Lovecraft himself still haunts these annual gatherings, as fans have reported everything from winds and snows that seemed timed to punctuate a reading,

PROVIDENCE

> *I read Lovecraft when I was a kid,*
> *And was so scared, for three weeks I hid.*
> *But it is a bit odd*
> *When a big elder god*
> *Has a head that looks just like a squid.*

to a murder of crows that arrived to observe and caw for a key part of the proceedings. If you'd like to attend the next H. P. Lovecraft Commemorative Service, you can call the H. P. Lovecraft Commemorative Activities Committee at (401) 732–4870 for details.

If you don't need all the pomp and circumstance but just want to visit the gravestone of H. P. Lovecraft, you can find it in Lot 5 at Swan Point Cemetery, 585 Blackstone Boulevard (401–272–1314). But note that taking photos of any of the headstones in this cemetery is not permitted, and that rule is strictly enforced.

FORGET ME NOT

Rhode Islanders are a stubborn people. We were the first to declare independence from Britain, and the last to join the thirteen colonies. And there's one holiday we continue to celebrate every August, in spite of the fact that nobody else has done so for decades. The holiday in question? Victory Day.

Victory Day, of course, is short for Victory over Japan Day, and commemorates the day when Emperor Hirohito announced that he would accept the terms of his county's surrender to the Allies. The date of the surrender was August 15, 1945, and was celebrated throughout the country with much fanfare and revelry as the end of World War II. Victory Day is still celebrated today as a holiday in Rhode Island on the second Monday of every August.

Where it isn't celebrated is anywhere else in the country. Other states still note the anniversary of the surrender quietly, but they no longer commemorate it with an official holiday. After all, Japan has been our ally for a number of years now, so there seems no reason to have an official holiday marking their defeat. It's been decades since any other state has celebrated Victory Day, with Arkansas being the most recent to remove it as a holiday, back in 1975. But Rhode Island will not give it up quietly—or at all. Suggestions that the holiday be eliminated have been met with such fervent opposition from Rhode Island veterans that few politicians would even dream of mentioning it today. Though some consider the day embarrassing and not politically correct, it maintains strong support, especially among the veterans.

Though "Victory Day" doesn't sound insulting, many Japanese Americans feel the implication of "Victory over Japan" is still too unpleasantly present. As a compromise measure, every few years some politician suggests not discarding the holiday, but merely changing its name to something less offensive, like "Peace and Remembrance Day" or "Rhode Island Veterans Day." And every time, that politician gets deluged with angry letters from veterans demanding that tradition be preserved and the name stay as the more descriptive "Victory Day." Thus, the holiday remains. In fact, it's a wonder that the official name was even toned down to Victory Day, given that most Rhode Islanders still refer to it as "VJ Day."

Regardless, Rhode Islanders all enjoy the extra day off from work, and the Rhode Island veterans who fought in the Second World War will not be moved when it comes to the name of their holiday. And to those who say celebrating Victory Day is inappropriate given our current alliance with Japan, Rhode Island asks you this: Do you celebrate Independence Day?

The Old Ball Game

If you ask the average Joe on the street who won baseball's first World Series, he won't know, because it was more than a century ago. If you ask the average baseball fan, he'll tell you that it was Boston, back in 1903. But if you ask an expert who really knows about baseball, he'll tell you that baseball's first World Series championship was won by the Providence Grays, in 1884. Sure, it wasn't technically called the World Series, because the term hadn't been coined yet, but the Grays' victory over the New York Metropolitans sealed their undisputed reputation as the world champions of baseball, for that year at least. After their 1885 season, the Providence Grays disbanded, and by the late twentieth century, it seemed as if baseball's first world champions and the game's history in Providence would soon be forgotten.

Enter one Tim Norton. In 1998 Norton attended a baseball historian's lecture about the Providence Grays, and that same year he saw an article about a vintage baseball league, where players followed the various nineteenth-century rules. This sparked a desire to resurrect the Providence Grays (the franchise and team name and baseball spirit, not the original players) as a vintage baseball team for a game against a New York vintage team, to honor the Grays' victory in 1884. Norton managed to gather enough people to field a team, and like many a Hollywood film, his ragtag band challenged the much more experienced New York team, all for the love for baseball.

But unlike most Hollywood films, the ragtag band of rookies were completely and utterly defeated by the New York veterans. Norton had gathered his players, played the big tribute game, and lost. But having finally re-created the glory of the Providence Grays, he wasn't about to stop. As pitcher and outfielder, Norton led the Grays through more than a hundred vintage baseball games. Vintage baseball may be similar to regular baseball, but some of the big differences are painfully obvious—

literally. The players do not protect themselves with such modern frip-peries as "gloves" or "helmets." So fielding a ball once it comes off the bat can be quite painful. The bats themselves are heavier than modern bats. And going even further than most vintage teams, the Providence Grays dress in wool uniforms, guaranteeing that any victory they earn will not only have blood and tears, but plenty of sweat as well.

While some may scoff at the eschewing of modern advancements, there is a majestic beauty in seeing things as they were originally meant to be. The Providence Grays play to win, but they play mainly for the love of the game. Instead of receiving millions of dollars like the major-league ballplayers, the Grays end up shelling out their own money just to play baseball. But it's totally worth it. If you attend a game played by the Providence Grays, you'll see a game with gentlemanly manners and a single baseball used for the whole game.

And you should attend. Watching a game is free, and you can find the schedule on their Web site at www.providencegrays.org. Although Norton stopped playing in 2004, he has remained on as president and helped the Grays play well over 200 games in the past eight years. They've become so popular that three other vintage baseball teams have popped up in Rhode Island. But none has the history of the Grays, who continue to do honor to the original franchise with their respect for the game. If you think you're man enough to join up with the Grays, drop an e-mail to Tim Norton at provgrays@yahoo.com. But if broken fingers from catching balls barehanded and running around in a wool uniform during summer's heat don't appeal to you, just show up to cheer them on. They'll still be glad to see you.

The Crowd Roars

The Roger Williams Park Zoo, at 1000 Elmwood Drive in Providence, is well-known as one of the best zoos in the country. While not as large as some zoos, it boasts a number of special features, including the carousel, the Japanese gardens, and the fact that it is situated in a beautiful park. They have lots of crowd-pleasing animals there as well, including penguins that waddle about, polar bears that dive into the water and press their paws on the glass where you can see them up close, and occasionally, dinosaurs.

That's right, dinosaurs.

Sure, they technically became extinct millions of years ago, but so did disco, and both occasionally manage to be revived on a small scale. In this case, the Roger Williams Park Zoo brings back the dinosaurs with a large exhibition of animatronic dinos that move, and roar, just like people imagined the real things might have. (The advantage of imitating a creature nobody has ever seen is that it's very difficult for people to conclusively prove that you've gotten something wrong.) With well over a dozen dinosaurs placed along the winding path, visitors to this exhibit can be awed by the large, loud lizards that loom overhead or lurk around the corner with gaping maws and gleaming teeth.

A collection of the resplendent robotic reptiles has been hosted by the zoo in 1992, 1994, 1997, 2000, 2005, and 2006. The cast is a rotating one, and has included long-necked vegetarian dinosaurs like the brachiosaur, famously fearsome carnivorous dinosaurs like the *Tyrannosaurus rex,* and a plethora of less famous dinosaurs like the cryolophosaur, which you have never heard of and will consequently mispronounce, thus incurring the mockery of the six-year-old boy who has memorized all of the dinosaur names.

Actually, the exhibition has changed somewhat over the years, in deference to the six-year-old dinosaur fans. The original exhibits showcased the dinosaurs in all of their gruesome glory, animatronically devouring the carcasses of other animals and generally earning their given name of "terrible lizards." It was a wonderful sight to behold, and I say that as someone who volunteered for a few months as a tour guide for the exhibit during the 1990s, timing my speeches to be perfectly punctuated by the various dinosaurs' mechanical roars which would cause little children to cling fearfully to their mother's leg. But the 2006 version of the exhibition was designed with the intent of *not* frightening the children, replacing the previous decade's bloody attempt at realism with a Hollywood theme.

Some zoos have endangered species, but Roger Williams has extinct species.

23

No, you can't see a real dinosaur,
There aren't any alive anymore.
But just come to the zoo,
And at least you can view
A mechanical one that will roar.

The dinosaur exhibition traditionally requires a small admission fee of less than $5.00 in addition to the zoo entrance fee, but since the 2006 exhibit has already closed, it's hard to say exactly what the price will be next time. Some have even said they're not sure if Roger Williams Park Zoo will ever host the dinosaurs again, but you can find out on their Web site at www.rogerwilliamsparkzoo.org or by calling (401) 785–3510. Either way, make plans to visit. It's a lovely zoo, even without the iguanadons. Still, there is hope that the dinosaurs will one day return once more. One can't really say the same about disco.

There's No Place Like Dome

While the Big Blue Bug is probably Rhode Island's most famous landmark, the State House runs a close second. It sits on Smith Hill in Providence, and although recent proximal construction has made it less visible from afar than it once was, it's still a beautiful sight to behold as you drive through Providence. The building was built more than a century ago, between 1895 and 1901, and looks like a miniature version of the U.S. Capitol building, probably due to all that marble. The Rhode Island State House consists of 327,000 cubic feet of white Georgia marble, as well as a few million bricks and well over a thousand tons of iron beams. But the real prize of the Rhode Island State House is the dome.

The glorious dome is round and beautiful and is topped by a large statue of a man. The Independent Man is a quarter-ton bronze statue covered in gold leaf, symbolizing the independent spirit that led to the founding of Rhode Island. But he's certainly not independent of the dome he's standing on, which is a good thing. And there are worse domes to be dependent on—the State House dome is even more famous than the Independent Man himself. At one point it was one of the top three unsupported domes of any kind in the world. Naturally, the world keeps building domes, but at present the dome still weighs in as the fourth-largest unsupported marble dome in the world. (The first three are St. Peter's Basilica in Rome, the Minnesota State Capitol, and the Taj Mahal in Agra, India, in that order.)

The statue is called the Independent Man, but he's pretty dependent on the dome to stand on.

But number four still ain't bad. The dome is 50 feet in diameter at its widest point, which is pretty darned impressive for a marble dome whose blocks are held together by nothing but tension and gravity. No beams, no mortar, just really good architecture and construction. Of course, great work like that doesn't come cheap. According to state records, building the State House ended up costing more than $3 million. And keep in mind, that's $3 million in 1900 dollars; it would be closer to $70 million these days.

For that price, not only does the outside of the dome have to impress, but the interior as well. Inside the dome is a mural called *The Four Freedoms,* which depicts four scenes from the lives of the settlers of Rhode Island: the Land Grant, Religious Tolerance, Pioneering and the Origins of Construction, and the Beginnings of Industry. *The Four Freedoms* would also be a catchy name for a musical group made up of the artists who painted the mural. It was originally designed and painted by James Allen King of Scituate, but he fell ill and was unable to finish his work, so he passed his sketches on to three other artists (George DeFelice, Robert C. Haun, and Victor Zucchi) to finish the job for him.

In addition to the mural, around the inside of the dome is carved a quote from the great Roman Tacitus that reads RARA TEMPORUM FELICITAS UBI SENTIRE QUAE VELIS ET QUAE SENTIAS DICERE LICET. Roughly translated, this means "Rare felicity of the times when it is permitted to think as you like and say what you think." An important thing to remember these days. Were you to lower your eyes yet more, you would see four medallions that depict Education, Justice, Literature, and Commerce. And if you looked down even further to the ground itself, in the middle of the rotunda lies the State Seal of Rhode Island. (And for those of you keeping track, that doesn't mean a dead otter. It's a brass representation of an anchor with the state motto, "Hope.")

So even if Rhode Islanders don't always agree with the laws that come out of the State House, they have to admire the work that went into it.

Self-guided tours are available Monday thru Friday from 9:00 A.M. to 3:00 P.M. To schedule a tour visit http://www.sec.state.ri.us/pubinfo/Tours/tourinfo.html or call the Secretary of State's office at (401) 222–2357.

Your Friendly Neighborhood Attorney General

One of the worst things about growing up is realizing that superheroes don't exist. Many of us spent our childhood following the adventures of the Justice League or similar superhuman defenders of truth and justice, and there was something glorious about them. But most of us, upon growing up, resigned ourselves to the harsh realities of life and abandoned the idea that these superheroes really stood for anything. Rhode Island attorney general Patrick Lynch, however, did not. In fact, upon taking office back in 2003, he installed a bronze plaque on his office building that quotes none other than the Amazing Spider-Man. The quote? "With great power comes great responsibility."

Lynch received a fair amount of resistance when he first suggested the quote. The state's previous attorney general, Sheldon Whitehouse, had set an example by selecting a much more classically grounded quote for his own 1999 assumption of the office. Whitehouse had installed a plaque quoting famed poet William Blake: "I will not cease from mental fight. Nor shall my sword sleep in my hand . . . " Lynch, however, wasn't much of a Blake fan. And more to the point, while Blake's poem may ring with power for the literati, the average passerby on the street is more likely to be caught in the web of a Spider-Man quote—or even the average kid on the street, which is how Lynch decided on the plaque. During his 2003 inauguration, Lynch's young son tugged on his pants and said, "Remember, with great power comes great responsibility."

Lynch was energized by the quote, which he felt perfectly encapsulated what the attorney general's office should stand for. His staff, upon hearing the quote, diligently researched it in the hope that Spider-Man had taken it from Shakespeare or some respectable ancient Greek source. But indeed, the quote belongs to Spider-Man, created by Stan Lee. Lynch was undeterred, and called up Marvel Comics to ask Stan Lee himself about proper attribution for the quote. In 2004 the plaque was installed at a public ceremony conveniently timed to coincide with the release of *Spider-Man 2*.

Evil-doers beware.

There are those who mock Lynch for his affinity for the web-slinger, but some have warmed to it. The lieutenant governor sent Lynch a framed print of Spider-Man swinging on a web in front of the State House, captioned with the immortal quote: "With great power comes great responsibility." Even former attorney general Sheldon Whitehouse says that he thinks the quote is a good fit for the attorney general's office. And Lynch continues to sling the quote whenever he gives speeches around the state, because it's something that everyone in his audience is likely to be able to connect to.

> We're not Gotham; no Batman to call,
> No Clark Kent to catch you if you fall.
> But you have to allow
> We can truly say now
> That we've got Spider-Man on our wall.

If you want to gaze upon this glorious statement in bronze, just swing by the outside of the attorney general's office at 150 South Main Street, the workplace of mild-mannered attorney general Patrick Lynch by day, and by night . . . who knows?

You Are What You Eat

If it's true that you can judge a person by what he or she eats, then the best place to truly learn about the human race is none other than the Culinary Museum and Archives at Johnson and Wales University on Harborside Boulevard (401–598–2805). It is America's biggest museum devoted to the history of the culinary and hospitality industries, which makes sense, as Johnson and Wales is the country's biggest university devoted to the culinary and hospitality industries. Heck, the museum has even been called "the Smithsonian of the food service industry." But while enrolling at the university to learn about the culinary industry will cost you roughly $20,000 a year, getting into the museum to learn all about the culinary industry will only cost you $7.00—$3.00 if you're a college student.

The only downside is that you won't see the private collection reserved for advanced scholarship and research. But since the collection includes literally hundreds of thousands of pieces of culinary history, even if you miss out on 50,000 cookbooks here or there, you'll hardly notice. If you try to see all the public collections, you'll already have bitten off more than you can chew. The huge museum building contains centuries of cooking history, everything from information on the New England tavern to a prodigious collection of kitchen gadgets through the ages. Food may go bad after a few weeks, but cooking tools from millennia past are still worth seeing. Or roll over to see more recent tools like the hollow glass rolling pins that were once filled with ice. There is even an exhibit on diners that includes the famed Worcester Diner car, showing how diners started in Rhode Island.

But what visitors hunger for the most is the presidential collection, with exhibits like History of the First Stomach and America the Bountiful that combine to cover pretty much everything that falls in the Venn diagram space between presidents and food. This includes campaigns

PROVIDENCE

(Hoover's slogan in 1928 was "a chicken in every pot"), presidential menus (Eisenhower cooked his own pancakes), dinner invitations, and even thank-you letters to constituents who sent turkey.

Interestingly, the Culinary Archives and Museum was not originally a museum. When founded in 1979, it was merely a library containing only a few thousand rare cookbooks. But ten years later, chef Louis Szathmary (of Chicago's famous restaurant The Bakery) donated many, many, many thousands of items from his personal collection. In fact, they are still trying to finish unpacking, cataloging, and storing all of the donations to this day. Several of the items in the museum are still unlabeled, so if you do decide to visit, you'd be well advised to take a guided tour from one of the university's students. And who knows? Twenty years from now, your tour guide may be a famous chef.

The hall of outmoded cookware.

Constant State of Mockery

Actually, Charlie Hall's Ocean State Follies specialize in constant mockery of state. This group of performers puts on shows that lampoon everything about Rhode Island from political scandals and current controversies to regional accents and notable figures. They dress up as big-haired girls named Cheryl and Rhonda from Cranston, pronouncing *Creeeeeeeeanston* with the nasal twang typical of that region. They sing parody songs ranging from the commercial snippet ("I want my Buddy back," to the tune of Chili's "I want my baby back ribs,"

Charlie Hall as former governor Bruce Sundlun, who became infamous for complaining about plasticware.

referring to former mayor Buddy Cianci, who was indicted and jailed), to the classic musicals ("East Side Story," about the east side of Providence), to the popular songs (Simon and Garfunkel surely never intended you to hear "Are you going to Scarborough Beach? Seaweed, gum, gold chains, and moussed hairs . . . ").

If it sounds like most of their material wouldn't be as funny if you don't live in Rhode Island, that's because most of their material wouldn't be as funny if you don't live in Rhode Island. The Follies have been voted the state's best comedy show of the year many times, so they entertain Rhode Islanders—or "Roe Dylinders," to be more accurate. If *youse* don't live here, *youse* might miss a lot of the jokes. But don't sweat: There are enough jokes in there that even if you miss 20 percent of them, you'll still have a good time. And not only is the patter between songs accessible to anyone, but they have a special segment explaining "Roe Dylandese" (or as they call it, "Rhodonics") to any unfortunate out-of-stater. After all, *langwich* is the key to *humah*.

It's worth mentioning that the group is called Charlie Hall's Ocean State Follies for a reason: Charlie Hall is the man behind it all. He's been performing as a stand-up comic for more than a quarter century and is

If there's one RI troupe you should hear,
It's the Ocean State Follies; that's clear.
They make fun of the state
From our hair to our great
Dialect, like "Wheah's Bob?" "No ideer!"

a cartoonist as well, but within the state he is best known as the creator of the Follies. Charlie is the man who writes the songs, the sketches, the jokes, and makes it all happen. He also sometimes performs in the shows, though the Follies have become so popular that there are a few different troupes of performers. And they appear at the oddest places, from jazz clubs to Italian restaurants.

People across the country make fun of Rhode Island all the time, usually asking if it's part of New York. But the Follies make fun of Rhode Island in a much more detailed and entertaining manner.

And lest you think Charlie doesn't love the state he so mercilessly mocks, he also wrote the lyrics for "Rhode Island's It for Me," a serious and beautiful piece which has now become the official state song. But usually he's still making fun of the state, because that's what he's best at.

Really, if you live in Rhode Island, you ought to see the Ocean State Follies at least once. Conveniently, you can plan this by visiting their Web site, www.oceanstatefollies.com.

Murphy's Slaw

When you want a good drink, you go to an Irish bar. When you want a good sandwich, you go to a Jewish deli. But where do you go when you want both? Oy vey, faith and begorra, you'd go to Murphy's Bar and Deli! Murphy's Bar and Deli, as you can probably tell from the name, is a combination bar and deli. Lying in the heart of Providence, it has for many years been a favorite lunching spot for employees of the *Providence Journal,* Rhode Island's biggest newspaper.

What you wouldn't know from the name is that the bar was originally

just called Murphy's Lunch. In 1950 Mr. Murphy met some Jews and added the deli, expanding the food offerings and making it a full bar and deli.

Lest you think a bar and deli is an odd combination, at one point it also included the Keyhole Lounge. But when the lounge fell apart, Murphy's took over the space, as well as the space of an old barbershop that moved out in 1978. Few people looking for haircuts still come by, but another of Murphy's old neighbors was Providence's famed joke shop, so some people still come looking for jokes.

What they find instead is Ruth Ferrazzano, who has owned Murphy's Deli for the past ten years. The previous owner made Murphy's mildly famous as a tri-national deli—a Greek owner of a Jewish deli with an Irish name. He even had a Greek flag adorned with a Star of David and a shamrock. But Ruth one-ups him, as the Jewish deli with an Irish name is now owned by a Swedish woman with an Italian name.

Ruth has actually worked at Murphy's since 1979, putting in eight years each for two different owners, making her the longest-serving waitress at the bar/deli by far. But after nearly two decades of working there, she decided it was time for a change. She had time to do things, and Murphy's seemed on the downslide, so she decided to open her own place.

Then in 1996 Ruth was looking in the classifieds and saw an ad that said "Pub for sale." She called to ask about the pub, and found that it was in Providence—what were the odds? When she asked where in Providence, and was astonished to learn that it was indeed the very pub she worked at that was for sale! As it turned out, Murphy's was going bankrupt, a new person had bought it, and that person was looking for a partner.

The rest is history. Ruth became the general manager and eventually the owner. And while the long trail from Murphy himself through a few other owners all the way to Ruth only has one other Irish owner, the spirit of the place remains.

While many improvements have been made since the 1970s, the feeling is the same, perhaps due to Ruth's philosophy of "Don't take away what works." She is always willing to try new things, but never willing to discard useful old ones. And it's good thing, too, because the Murphy's Reuben (their signature sandwich) remains extremely tasty—just like my memories of it from ten years ago. A deli, a bar, some TV screens . . . what more do you want?

Oh, an address. Well, since 1929 Murphy's Bar and Deli has been at 55 Union Street. But in May 2007 Ruth moved to 100 Fountain Street. Either way, it's still right in the middle of Providence, and surely delicious.

Murphy's Reuben: This sandwich, in chief,
Contains sauerkraut, cheese, and corned beef.
Just squeeze on Russian dressing,
And then you'll be blessing
The gods as you sink in your teef.

Letter Rip

If you're a stamp collector, you should try to collect a commemorative stamp from the opening of the world's first fully automated post office. If you're not a stamp collector, don't worry about it—after all, they say philately will get you nowhere. But at the very least, you should know that said post office was built in Providence. Back in 1958 the United States Postmaster General decided that the world's first entirely automated post office should be built in Rhode Island. The contract was drawn up and assigned to Intelex Systems in 1959. After testing a few machines in Washington, D.C., the post office finally opened in 1960.

Sure, it looks innocent now. But back in the day, it was on a tear.

The machinery was nothing if not impressive. The building boasted nearly 16,000 feet of conveyer belts, overseen by a giant 25-foot-high control tower. The machines could handle nearly 25,000 letters an hour by funneling all the mail through one of six culling machines which separated the letters and cards by size. Other machines scanned the letters for stamps, flipping them over if necessary, and cancelled the stamps, sending the letters back out in neat little stacks. This marvel of modern machinery was a complete triumph of technology.

At least, that's how the history books might present it. Providence residents at the time, however, had a less flattering nickname for the country's first automated post office: the Mangler. New technology never works entirely smoothly, and in spite of the few tests in Washington, D.C., the Intelex postal machines were no exception. Consequently, some letters sent through this newfangled automated post office came back a little torn—or more than a little torn. It was not uncommon at that time to go to your mailbox and find some pieces of a letter in a plastic bag, and there was little to be done except to

We told 'em "Deliver de letter,"
We told 'em "De sooner de better."
But de letter came torn.
Maybe next time, we'll warn:
"Keep de letter away from de shredder!"

shake your head and say, "Ah, the Mangler." Considering the fact that this was the 1960s and the new machinery was handling roughly seventy pieces of mail per second, in retrospect it's no great surprise that many letters ended up torn, shredded, or mangled. But that's what you get for pushing the envelope.

PROVIDENCE

A Herculean Task

What's an even harder city improvement project than moving a road? Moving a river. And what's an even harder city improvement project than moving a river? Moving two rivers, of course! Providence, for many years, wasn't sure what to do with its rivers. They had been befouled for decades by sewage and industrial waste, to the point where the water was closer to brown than blue. And by the middle of the twentieth century, it had gotten so bad that Providence had covered them up altogether—with highways, parking lots, and the world's widest bridge.

Some have argued that the Crawford Street Bridge wasn't really a bridge because was just a bunch of concrete decking extending over the water. Those people must not know that most bridges *are* concrete that spans water, so they can go jump in a murky river. The Crawford Street Bridge was, for a time, the widest bridge in the world. It covered more than two acres of waterway. So there. However, it stood in the middle of a congested city. The murky rivers had been covered up with concrete that created a murky traffic flow, including a rotary that some residents called "Suicide Circle." Something had to be done.

Since the project was ultimately a success, everyone is quick to claim credit, but it's hard to know who really deserves it. Mayor Buddy Cianci did run Providence at the time. Ken Orenstein was looking for an alternative to the first suggested solution to the traffic problem, which was paving over even more river. William Warner got a $100,000 grant to study the possibility of restoring the rivers to their former glory, and beyond; his fantasy was backed up by many slide shows of what Providence could be. And various other characters touted the merits of reopening rivers, like James Rouse, designer of Boston's Quincy Marketplace waterfront.

Still, regardless of who started Providence's renewal project, it took many people, many years, and many millions of dollars to complete it.

The Crawford Street Bridge was ripped up, a dozen new bridges were built, and roads were rerouted. But there was a snag: A post office at the junction of the Woonasquatucket and Moshassuck Rivers could not be moved. When Muhammad won't come to the mountain, there's only one thing to be done: The rivers were redirected. So, two rivers moved, one world's widest bridge destroyed, $88 million spent, countless new roads laid out, a decade or two, and voila! Rivers moved, city revitalized. Waterplace Park, located on Memorial Boulevard between the Providence Place mall and Exchange Street crossing, has since become a cultural mecca, with many pedestrians now enjoying the area that symbolizes Providence's renaissance, even when there's not a Water-Fire celebration. And the traffic flows better. And the water's prettier. All in all, a smashing success.

Besides, who needs the world's widest bridge anyway?

Whatever Floats Your Boat

When some cities say they have a renaissance, they just mean that they rebuilt things a little. But when Providence has a renaissance, they have a full-blown Italian Renaissance. And that means including the best of Venice—like a gondola. Sure, any city could technically buy a gondola, but they wouldn't have a place to put it, and it wouldn't fit thematically. Before the Providence renaissance, the city had no place for a gondola either. But after ripping up two acres of concrete decking, moving two rivers, and creating new bridges, Providence was a city revitalized. More than revitalized, it was renaissanced.

Since then the middle of Providence has borne a more-than-passing resemblance to Venice. Long, narrow rivers now flow through the city, with lots of cobblestone walkways for pedestrians, and everything you see from the water is beautiful because the cars are generally more than a dozen feet above the river level. So when would a gondola grace this new aquatic paradise? It was just a matter of Days—Marco and Cynthia Days, to be specific. In 1996 they hired a New England boat-builder to make an authentic replica of a nineteenth-century gondola, believed to be the first of its kind ever built in the United States. But the quest for authenticity (combined with the unexpected popularity of the first gondola) led the Days to order a second gondola directly from Italy. How's that for authentic? And naturally, both gondolas are black, in accordance with the 1562 Venetian law. If you're going to have a renaissance, you want to do it right.

Each gondola seats six passengers, measures 36 feet in length, and weighs more than three-quarters of a ton. The boats have red upholstered seats, colorful carpets, and enough brass trim and red

Providence may have the most authentic Italian culture anywhere but Italy.

cording to make you think Venetian royalty wouldn't mind riding in one—but only if there was a good driver, because while it may look simple to stand on a gondola and move it around, it takes a lot of practice. Gondolas are flat on the bottom and have no keel for balance or steering. In a time of motorboats and super-crafted aerodynamic kayaks, gondolas remain a giant flat boat steered and powered by one man wielding nothing but a 14-foot-long oar. Well, almost nothing. Marco Days also wears the traditional gondolier costume of blue-and-white-striped shirt, black pants, and straw hat. Perhaps this is what gives him a Venetian mastery over the gondola as he steers it through Providence's rivers.

Sound romantic? Sure it is. Heck, in 1998 it was voted the best place to pop the question. You can even ask Marco to sing if you really want, though you should know that Venetian gondoliers don't sing very often, so it's more authentic if you just sit back and enjoy the view. If you're lucky enough to reserve a spot during WaterFire, you won't need things to be any more romantic anyway. But despite the love they inspire in most people, there's always someone tossing out hate. Sadly, the gondolas were vandalized in 2003, but Providence mayor David Cicilline met with the Days and offered assistance so they could have their boats restored and running again.

They're back in full swing now, and La Gondola continues to thrive due mainly to a man, a plan, and a canal. So if you want to guarantee a spot on the gondola for yourself, a paramour, or up to six people total, you should probably call and make reservations. (It'll cost you a little more if you want to go out during WaterFire, but it's totally worth it.) And you can even bring your own wine to drink as you're floating on the rivers of Providence for a half hour. Now that's what I call authenticity. La Gondola's season runs from May through October; call (401) 421–8877 or visit www.gondolari.com for details.

The Sauciest Mayor in America

Vincent "Buddy" Cianci made lots of headlines during his five terms as mayor of Providence. Part of this was because he was such a publicity hound that he would attend the opening of a letter, and part of this was because, let's face it, he did a lot of crazy stuff. But while some of his actions while in office may have left a bad taste in people's mouths, he did leave a legacy with a bit more taste—his own brand of marinara sauce.

How can a mayor sell sauce while in office? Simple: by donating all proceeds to charity. Back in 1991 Cianci created the Vincent A. Cianci Jr. Scholarship Fund, which gives $1,000 college scholarships to Providence high school students unable to receive

You can indict him and take away his office, but you can't beat his sauce.

Italian Style Sauce with Old World Charm

Vitamin C
No Cholesterol
100% Pure Olive Oil

Net. Wt.
26 oz.

Former Mayor Vincent A. Cianci, Jr. TM
THE **MAYOR'S OWN MARINARA SAUCE**
Benefiting Providence School Children

43

Pell grants. In addition to the academic criteria, recipients must demonstrate involvement in the Providence community. After all, if there's one thing Cianci believed in above everything else, it was improving Providence. Fast forward a few years, to a press conference in 1994. Cianci had mixed a batch of sauce to give away at one of his events, but had a few jars of leftovers sitting on his desk during the press conference. Reporters were curious about the sauce, and after the articles came out, people starting calling to ask where they could buy it.

Cianci, like his sauce, wasn't thick. He recognized the opportunity and created the Mayor's Own Marinara Sauce, complete with his own face and the Providence Mayoral Seal on the label. After giving a few jars away to visiting famous figures like Bill Clinton, he began convincing a few local markets to sell it, with all proceeds going to the scholarship fund. Pretty soon he found distributors and began getting the sauce sold all over Rhode Island—including in the T. F. Green Airport gift shop, as a souvenir. The Mayor's Own Marinara Sauce was covered by *USA Today* and even *The Today Show*.

So what's in it? Well, the Mayor's Own Marinara Sauce is a variation on an old family recipe, and with a family name like Cianci, you know it's Italian (although the fact that he's named Vinny should have helped, too). Like many marinara sauces, it contains tomatoes, onions, garlic, olive oil, and herbs. Two big differences are that Cianci insists that marinara sauce should be thin and not chunky, and it contains carrots to cut the acidity of the tomatoes. He must have done something right with the recipe, because it won a blind taste test for the state's best jarred spaghetti sauce.

Even though he has been indicted and imprisoned, the sauce continues to be sold as "Mayor's Own." And the Vincent A. Cianci Jr. Scholarship Fund is still going strong. You can take a man's office and you can take away his freedom, but you can't take away his marinara sauce.

Such a Pest

There are a number of famous landmarks in Rhode Island, from the statue of Roger Williams to the State House dome. But the most famous Rhodey landmark of all is no historical figure or government architectural feat. No, the landmark known to more Rhode Islanders than any other is a gigantic two-ton termite known as the Big Blue Bug.

It's impossible to miss the Big Blue Bug, perched atop New England Pest Control headquarters, overlooking Interstate 95 in the middle of Providence. After all, when a 9-foot-high, 58-foot-long wire-mesh and fiberglass termite is looming 30 feet over your car, it's hard to ignore. And hard to ignore is precisely what businessman Leonard Yale Goldman wanted.

In 1979 Goldman's company, New England Pest Control, purchased a small building on an insignificant little street between Allens Avenue and Eddy Street. In order to announce their presence, they decided to commission a gigantic termite from the Avenia Sign Company in Providence. In October 1980, amid high winds, the termite was installed conspicuously atop the building, and began to draw ever-increasing attention.

Rhode Island's most famous landmark: Nibbles Woodaway.

Of course, after driving by it twice a day for a few years, people became used to the prodigious pest. So in 1995 New England Pest Control decided to rekindle interest, and began a tradition of dressing the bug for the holidays. If there's one thing more eye-catching than a two-ton termite, it's a two-ton termite in a witch's hat, or a two-ton termite decked out with antlers, a bright red Rudolph nose, and hundreds of feet of Christmas lights (and you thought doing costumes for your kids was pricey and time-consuming).

The Big Blue Bug is *the* essential Rhode Island icon. A local radio station held a contest in 1990 to name the bug, and Nibbles Woodaway was the winning entry. Nonetheless, most people still refer to it as "The Big Blue Bug." In 2002 the bug was taken down to be repainted and to take a small tour. It's said that the bug was originally purple (the actual color of termites) before the sun bleached it blue, but the repainting was undeniably a deep blue, thus keeping the Big Blue Bug tradition alive. The Big Blue Bug has appeared in numerous movies, but fame has not gone to its head: It has remained vigilantly atop New England Pest headquarters, and shows no sign of taking wing.

Midnight Snack

The best way to explain the charm of the Haven Brothers Diner is with this absolutely true story: Many years ago, my grandparents went on their very first date. My grandfather knew a lot about Providence, and so he took my grandmother to Haven Brothers for dinner. Nothing fancy, just good ol' burgers and dogs and fries. My grandmother really enjoyed it, so the next day she called up a few of her friends and brought them over to see the diner where she'd just had a date. When they arrived at the spot, there was no diner there at all, and my grandmother was mystified. What she didn't know is that the Haven Brothers

Diner doesn't pull into the spot next to city hall until roundabouts 5:00 P.M. The diner is open from 5:00 P.M. until 3:00 A.M., and then packs up and drives away until 5:00 P.M. the next night. And it's been doing so for more than a century.

Providence may be the birthplace of diners in general, but few are as well-known as Haven Brothers, which began back in the late nineteenth century when Anna Coffey Haven opened a horse-drawn lunch wagon that would serve food at the corner of Dorrance Street. The horse-drawn cart was

The Haven Brothers Diner: Here today, gone tomorrow morning.

soon replaced with a shiny diner, and the business was passed down in the Haven family until 1953 when they sold it to Albert Mollicone. But the diner wagon they sold him is the same one that operates today, bought from the Fred W. Morse Company (a Providence diner manufacturer) back in 1949.

In 1986 Mollicone sold the business to Jack Ferry (who had worked there for ten years) and Saverio Giusti, and the Giusti family continues to run the diner today—which is not to say it's been all smooth sailing. Various city officials have tried to have the diner relocated ever since it took up residence next to city hall, but the people's love for Haven Brothers overcame all opposition. As far back as 1926, some felt that the location was undignified and the Board of Aldermen considered moving the Haven Brothers lunch cart, but it was so popular that nobody wanted to have their name associated with the order. He who steals my purse steals trash, but he who steals my food will never be reelected.

It's true. When taxes rise, people accept it, but in 1986 when Providence mayor Joe Paolino declared that the Haven Brothers Diner did not fit in with the new modernized Providence, there was an uproar. Paolino's office was deluged with calls and letters from residents demanding that this Providence institution remain. Talk radio was swamped with calls from listeners who couldn't abide the death of the tradition. And even many of Paolino's own political supporters declared their steadfast support for Haven Brothers. Paolino eventually listened to reason, and allowed the diner to remain. His mayoral successor (and predecessor), Buddy Cianci, was always a very strong supporter of Haven Brothers—as well as a frequent diner!

So what is it about the diner that inspires such loyalty? The food is comforting: plump greasy chili dogs, cheese-covered french fries, hot baked beans, and the house special Murder Burger, which is a double cheeseburger with chili, bacon, mushrooms, onions, lettuce, tomatoes, and mayonnaise. But more than the food, the clientele at Haven Brothers is a microcosm of the city. Everyone from suit-wearing politicians to biker gang members to young college kids to old drunken hippies all eat at Haven Brothers. And there's really something magnificent about a diner where everyone feels at home, and has for more than a hundred years.

> Haven Brothers: A delicacy,
> Greasy food all night long until 3.
> But heed you this warning:
> Show up in the morning,
> And asphalt is all that you'll see.

If you decide to take the trip to Haven Brothers, you can find them in their reserved parking spot on the corner of Fulton and Dorrance Streets, right in front of city hall, from 5:00 P.M. to 3:00 A.M. every day. With only a handful of stools in the diner, chances are you'll end up taking your food outside to eat on the curb or steps of city hall, especially since the stools tend to fill up fast. But remember not to show up for lunch, because they won't just be closed, they won't even be there at all.

Smoke on the Water

Providence's rivers used to be somewhat polluted, though never to the point where a whole river caught fire, like in Cleveland. Still, now that Providence has been all cleaned up, you can go down to the river on some evenings and see lots of fire on the water. This time, however, it's on floating torches, as part of the Water-Fire celebrations at Water-place Park.

What is WaterFire?

WaterFire: a combination of water and fire. Who'd have guessed?

Well, descriptions really don't do it justice, but since you're reading this book and presumably not currently standing at WaterFire, here goes. WaterFire began as a fire-sculpture installation by artist Barnaby Evans, who took torches of fire and installed them along the water, as you might guess from the name. The First Fire took place in 1994, commissioned as part of Providence's tenth annual First Night celebration on New Year's Eve. Evans created the Second Fire for an International Sculpture Conference two years later, and his work was so popular that Rhode Islanders organized a fund-raising effort to keep it happening through a nonprofit foundation.

Now WaterFire happens nearly twenty times a year, with a series of bonfires just above the water in specially constructed braziers along parts of the Providence River and two of its tributaries, the Woonasquatucket and the Moshassuck. The braziers are filled with a mixture of pine, oak, and cedar, which creates a surprisingly pleasant aroma. Though it started with only a few braziers, the number was raised to forty-two in 1997, eighty-one in 1998, ninety-seven in 1999, and now there are three more for an even hundred. As the number of fires has grown, so has the number of fans. And as the fans grow, so do the number of fires. You could say they're fanning the flames.

The fires look magnificent reflecting off of the water, whether you're viewing them from a bridge above, a walkway on the river, or a gondola floating right by the flames. The braziers in a line come to a large circle at the hub of Waterplace Park, which many have called the heart of Providence's renaissance. But the fires are only the beginning. Water-Fire also always has music selected by designer Barnaby Evans to complement the flames. And in addition to the main music on the river, there is also a plethora of other events around. Live jazz music and ballroom-dancing demonstrations are just two of the more common installations. There are also fighting demonstrations, living gargoyles, and various other amusements depending on the day.

With a crowd of many tens of thousands of people, WaterFire is essentially Providence's giant block party. And the best part is, it's free and you're invited! WaterFire can survive passing storms and small showers, but if the weather looks dire, it's sometimes cancelled. Otherwise, the fires are lit at sunset, and the party goes all night long. To check up on when the next WaterFire is, whether it's cancelled, and what special entertainments will be there, you can call their information line at (401) 272–3111 or visit www.waterfire.org.

The 3-H Club

You're probably familiar with the 4-H Club, which consists of a bunch of young do-gooders helping their community. But if you drop down to 3-H, you've got a much older group that tends to have a different kind of fun: the Hash House Harriers. The Rhode Island Hash House Harriers (RIH3) describe themselves as "the drinking club with a running problem," which should give you a very clear picture of the two most important parts of being a Hash House Harrier.

There are other Hash House Harrier clubs, but there's no central command, so it's not really a big organization. In fact, it's more like a disorganization. Anyway, the important thing is that the RIH3 make their own rules, and have their own individual names—names like Basket Boom Boom and Dry Foot Fairy, and often less appropriate ones like Amish It Head. The RIH3 club meets every Monday for a "hash," which is what they call their runs. The hash was started in Kuala Lampur, Malaysia, back in 1938, and it basically consists of two main things: drinking and running.

Of course, it's slightly more complicated than that. The run begins with one runner (called the "hare") who lays out a trail of a few miles for the other runners, by use of various markings. The rest of the runners, after giving the hare a fifteen-minute head start, set out in an attempt to follow the trail, which likely consists of a few false leads, circles where the next part of the trail isn't immediately clear, and various other tricky things. The trail also generally contains a beer stop in the middle of the run, where the runners can stop and drink a brew, and always includes a larger (lager?) beer stop at the end of the run, where all the hashers drink beer in a circle, in accordance with ancient hashing ritual. While following the trail, runners yell out "On, on!" to lead others toward correct trails, and during the final drinking circle, people yell "Down, down!" as some of the hashers must down their entire beer in the center of the circle.

Dr. WHO, just another horny hash house harrier.

And that's your basic Hash House Harrier run. Naturally, the Rhode Island Hash House Harriers have their own traditions. Every year, on the Monday nearest Robert Burns Day, they have a Robert Burns run where all of the runners wear kilts. The RIH3 also has a collection of their own songs, which they sing at hashes while drinking. Some of the songs describe the RIH3 members, and most of them are unprintable, but here's a brief snippet by Basket Boom Boom that isn't R-rated: "A little beer, a down-down here. I had to guzzle, now I feel queer. I'm no physician, it's my suspicion: Rhode Island Hashin'."

I first encountered the Rhode Island Hash House Harriers all dressed in Viking costumes, and spoke with RIH3 member Dr. WHO (the WHO stands for yet more unprintable words). When he first explained the concept of the hash, I asked him why the hash was always on a Monday, and he explained that Hash House Harriers traditionally drink on Monday to deal with the weekend hangover from Sunday. One might think drinking so much on Monday might cause problems, too, but Dr. WHO's response to that was simple: "Worry about that on Tuesday."

The Rhode Island Hash House Harriers have been going strong for more than a decade and show no signs of stopping, except, of course, for a few beers. The weekly hash continues every Monday and always welcomes newcomers, so if you're of age and want to join the RIH3, you can e-mail Basket Boom Boom at basketboomboom@cox.net or call him at (401) 568–3157.

Chairmen of Charity

Some people run for charity. For those who want to help a charity but aren't quite in shape enough to run fast over long distances, there are jog-a-thons. For those who aren't even in shape enough to jog, there are walk-a-thons. And if even a walk-a-thon would be too physically taxing for you, you still have no excuse not to help the Obscure Company raise money for cancer at their annual sit-a-thon.

That's right, sit-a-thon. Every year members of the Obscure Company and other volunteers sit down for charity, and keep their butts in seats for twelve hours to raise money for a good cause. The 2006 event took place at Goddard Park, with roughly thirty sitters being actively sedentary for a good cause. The sitters are allowed four bathroom breaks over the twelve-hour period, but other than that, their butts remain in their chairs.

The Obscure Company takes a stand for not standing.

Which is not to say that nothing is going on. Far from it. People are reading, chatting, and playing various games. Snacks and drinks flow freely, and various toys are strewn about the tables. Musicians and magicians have even come in to entertain the sitters. And sometimes sitting down doesn't have to mean sitting still: I have witnessed at least one chair race with two people scooting their chairs backwards as fast as they could go. All in all, it's probably more fun than you had the last time you were standing. Best of all, it's for a good cause.

So what kind of people decide that the best way to raise money for charity is to sit? Well, the Obscure Company now consists of eight volunteer staff members led by president John Colwell, but basically began as a few bored teens in school. They enjoyed doing random things, and one fateful day in 1999 took a chair and a couch and sat on the median strip of a highway all day long. They decided to form a company based around doing odd things. "We wanted people to know us, but not know why they know us," says Colwell. Various names were tossed around, but the Obscure Company stuck.

The Obscure Company continues to grow, and became an official charity in 2006. This means that donations to them are all tax-deductible, so you should make some. They host other events like the winter chestnut roast, but their flagship event remains the sit-a-thon. They've raised thousands of dollars for various charities, and none of it through normal fund-raising events. "We enjoy raising money for a good cause in strange ways," Colwell explains. If you like the idea of raising money for charity, but are too lazy to raise a finger, you don't have to: Just show up next year and sit.

To donate to the Obscure Company, view a calendar of upcoming events, or just learn more about the crazy people who came up with the idea, visit www.obscurecompany.com.

Class Clowns

Clowning around in class will often get you in trouble during school, but not clowning around in class could get you in trouble after school, if you were taking after-school classes from the Providence Circus School. The school has been running since 1998, under the metaphorical big tent of the What Cheer Art Company. As you might expect, they teach circus arts, ranging from juggling with balls, scarves, rings, and clubs, to acrobatics like somersaults, rolls, and flips. As you might not expect, in addition to classes at their base in Providence, they tour around the state and provide after-school guest classes at various locations across Rhode Island.

The founder of all this? Judy Plotz, whose last name sounds like the landing you might make

Providence Circus School: Join the club, club, club.

if you weren't skilled in acrobatics. But she is—Plotz has studied yoga and dance, in addition to the usual circus arts like balance skills and juggling. After learning a lot from Vermont's Circus Smirkus, she decided that Rhode Island should have a circus school, too. And now it does; you could say she has fulfilled her circus *in-tent*.

In addition to the classes, where kids can learn serious clowning, the Providence Circus School offers special workshops with famous circus performers, participates in festivals at schools and libraries, and even teaches circus skills to teachers. After all, if you have to deal with twenty kids, there's a lot of juggling required. But it's mostly children who take the classes.

Of course, being a clown isn't for everyone. So if you'd prefer to just watch other people tumbling and tossing, you can catch a show by their performance troupe, Lub-Dub. Lub-Dub began in 2003 and has performed at various libraries, festivals, and even a children's hospital. The group features instructors from the circus school like program coordinator Michaela Andrews, who has been teaching juggling and acrobatics for five years. She was a member of the Brown Juggling Club (where she probably threw brown juggling clubs), and now performs all sorts of juggling in addition to plate-spinning and poi-twirling.

If watching one of their performances stokes the squirting flower of your heart, or if you've got a would-be clown, you can reach the Providence Circus School, which is located at 104 Eleventh Street, by calling (401) 351–9211 or e-mailing jplotz@aol.com.

Bridge over Troubled Water

I feel sorry for the people who only see the Providence River Bridge now. Seeing a giant 5.5-million-pound bridge over the Providence River isn't terribly unusual. After all, that's what giant bridges are for, spanning bodies of water. But those who were around in the autumn of 2006 got to see a 5.5-million-pound bridge on water. Not over, on. As in, slowly but surely floating down the river—or technically, up the river. Who cares? It was a giant 5.5-million-pound bridge, floating on barges on the river.

Most people just build bridges where they want them, but the network arch bridge that would cross the Providence River was going to be 80 feet high, 400 feet long, and very, very heavy. The decision was made to build the bridge in North Kingstown first and then float it in. And while this is highly irregular, there were good reasons for it. The piers that would hold the arch were not completed on schedule, so building the arch separately allowed construction of both to take place at the same time. And building a bridge isn't easy. Building it at Quonset Point in North Kingstown meant flat ground, lots of space, and no rigging. Building it in place would have meant that any falling pieces would have sunk, and many temporary supports would have been needed at added time and expense (not to mention the danger of damaging the underground sewer line). Cranes couldn't even fit into the spaces needed to work on the bridge on-site.

Thus it was that a pair of 300-foot-long barges, the *Chesapeake Trader* and the *Atlantic Trader,* spent the better part of a day floating the Providence River Bridge 12 miles from Quonset Point to Providence. For those who were there to see the bridge float up the river, it was a sight to behold. But perhaps the bridge was most interesting for those Rhode Islanders who were away for the weekend. When they left, there were only supports, and when they returned, a giant arch bridge spanned the Providence River. It must have looked like the fastest construction job ever, but chances are that someone barged in and told them the truth.

The bridge was designed by architect William D. Warner and engineer Patricia D. Steere to not only look nice against the Providence background, but also to provide lots of support without needing too much steel. So, 5.5 million pounds was the light version of what the bridge could have been. Light version or not, it's probably not a bridge you should eat if you're on a diet.

Bug Bites

David Gracer has the food bug. Actually, he has a lot of food bugs, and he'd like you to have some food bugs too. Gracer is the man behind Sunrise Land Shrimp, and is trying to bring the eating of insects back into the common culture. More specifically, he'd like to bring entomophagy (eating insects) into American culture, since many other countries around the world already eat insects, especially throughout Asia and Africa. Even fancy European menus used to feature insects, but they have become less popular in the last few centuries. Still, as America goes culturally, so goes the world, and thus Dave Gracer has a clear mission to show them the light—even if that light has a few dead bugs that got stuck in it.

Gracer gives shows at various nature centers and schools to introduce people to the wonderful world of insect eating. He generally gives a talk, leads a walk to catch a few things, holds a question-and-answer session, and then offers up some tasty bugs. Half of the audience is usually kids, who Gracer hopes will learn to discover things for themselves. Convincing Americans to ignore their cultural conditioning isn't easy. There's definitely an "ick" factor, explains Gracer, which causes

most Americans to recoil and say "Ewwwwwww!" at the idea of eating bugs. But insects have good pharmacological properties, lots of protein, and are probably more environmentally friendly to eat than whatever you're eating now. In fact, if eating insects was something seen regularly on TV, there's little doubt that people would consider it normal.

David Gracer of Sunrise Land Shrimp. Not just a fly-by-night operation—he also has cicadas.

Perhaps this is why one of Gracer's dreams is to have insects as a steady diet for a full month. It would be similar to the movie *Super Size Me,* about a man eating nothing but McDonald's for a month, only much healthier. "I wanted to find a sufficient variety of insects and culinary techniques to make them the centerpiece of my meal for thirty days," says Gracer. Sadly, finding a variety of insects is trickier than you might expect. For example, crickets and mealworms are easy enough to get at pet stores, as long as you don't announce what you want them for. Many places won't sell insects to people who say they plan to eat them, but are happy to sell them if they presume you're feeding them to your pets.

Surprisingly, Gracer was somewhat of a finicky eater as a child. He was an environmentalist and went wild mushroom hunting, but certainly did not grow up eating bugs (at least not on purpose). In 1999 a friend of his gave him some flavored mealworm snacks. Gracer, though not impressed by the taste, was intrigued. After attending a presentation by insect advocate David Gordon, Gracer was converted. He got some images from a show in New York and began doing his own presentations. It started at the Entomological Society of America meeting in spring 2003, and although he only does a few shows a year at present, he hopes to do more.

A great protein for not too much money,
Bugs are crunchy and taste good with honey.
But as Dave Gracer knows,
When you're chewing on those,
People often will look at you funny.

On the home front, Gracer has a freezer that is completely stuffed with various boxes and bags of frozen insects. He was even kind enough to fry me up some cicadas, crickets, and water bugs—the first two making a tasty snack, the latter tasting like salty fruit. Gracer's favorite insect to eat is the katydid. His wife, alas, dislikes eating insects, but also dislikes crab. People allergic to shellfish tend to also be allergic to insects, because the two have a lot of similarities; hence the name of his company, Sunrise Land Shrimp. However, insists Gracer, "Crickets eat much better than lobsters."

If you'd like to learn more about eating insects, and aren't too afraid to try some land shrimp, drop David Gracer a line at dave@slshrimp.com or visit his Web site at www.slshrimp.com. Best of all, you don't even have to pretend it's for your pet.

Quoth the Raven

If you wanted to hear stories about Edgar Allan Poe's old haunts, you'd probably ask a raven. And when it comes to both Poe and haunting places, no raven knows more than the mysterious Rory Raven. Rory Raven is a man with a serious interest in the paranormal, supernatural, psychic, and so forth. He has always been fascinated by what he refers to as "the weird," and has spent a lot of time studying it (some might even say, being it).

Eventually, Rory Raven made a career as a mentalist. What's a mentalist? Well, it's like a mind reader, except for the fact that he doesn't claim to read anyone's mind. He produces the same results, regardless, so his audiences rarely complain. Performing theater of the mind lets him get on stage and divine people's thoughts to the extent that regardless of whether you believe in telepathy or not (and he himself doesn't), one can't help but find the performance interesting. But Raven's interest in the mind and the paranormal doesn't stop there. He also has extensively studied the ghost stories of the Providence area.

Years ago Raven went to Newport and saw a ghost tour there. He felt it was obvious that Providence ought to have one, too, and was surprised that it didn't. But he didn't cry about it. He studied up even more on the ghost stories of the area and created the Providence Ghost Walk, which he has led since the turn of this century. Dressed in a mildly spooky black tux with cape, top hat, and wooden cane, he starts his ghost walks from the Providence Athenaeum. And what better place? Poe spent much time there when he was alive. In fact, there are some who say Poe spends much time there now, walking the upper floors in ghostly form.

The ever-dapper Rory Raven, dressed in black like his namesake.

PROVIDENCE

And if there's a ghost story in Providence, Rory Raven probably knows about it. He has not only done lots of reading up on Poe as well as other local ghost stories, but collects tales that have been told for years and folklore from whispered corners. His favorite stories, he says, are the old ones that have been long forgotten, like that of the ghostly lamplighter on the street, appearing mysteriously at night. Then again, he's been known to mix the ancient stories with his own tales. "I invented one of the stories I'll tell today," says Raven at the beginning of his Providence Ghost Walk. "But I won't say which one."

Not that Raven needs to do much inventing of stories, given how much he has researched. In addition to studying lots of local folklore and hearing countless ghost stories, he does his own investigating, having asked the people at each haunted site to share their tales. When they had none to tell, he managed to scare up their neighbors. All this adds up to a lot of ghostly knowledge for Rory Raven, who not only can show you the most haunted sites in Providence, but also can quote you various verse while doing so, and is even willing to share a few good epitaphs of which he knows.

The only thing he's not filled with information about is himself. Though he can tell you about the buried bodies behind the shunned house, don't expect an answer if you ask him whether Rory Raven is his real name. He'll just direct you to his Web site at www.roryraven.com. But all you really need to know is that on any weekend afternoon in October, if you manage to drop by the Providence Athenaeum when the clock strikes three, you can take the Providence Ghost Walk. Unless you're too afraid . . .

LICENSE TO THRILL

If you aren't from Rhode Island, you may not think there's anything special about low-number license plates. And you may be a fool. Because in Rhode Island, low-numbered plates are worth their weight in gold. While families elsewhere may pass down shiny rocks through the generations, in Rhode Island the greatest thing one can leave their children is a low-number license plate. Vanity plates don't count, but if you are lucky enough to have a Rhode Island plate with four digits or less, it is a sign of great status, likely passed down or paid highly for. Richard Dragon even wrote a book called *Registered in R.I.* about the state's obsession with license plates, explaining how Rhode Islanders always want to get lower-number plates for higher status.

It's not entirely insane: Low-number plates have always been associated with connections, be they political friends or rich family. And people have been wheeling and dealing to get them ever since the very first plate—literally. In 1904, when Rhode Island first issued license plates, the number 1 plate was given to a Dr. Rowland Robinson, in gratitude for his brother's (senator Benjamin Robinson) help in passing an automobile-registration bill. Since then low-number plates have continued to be favors. Longtime Rhode Islanders tell of how you used to be able to buy them by donating to the right politician. When Bruce Sundlun became governor in 1991, his office vowed to issue low-number plates in order without bias, and when he left office, he was berated for approving the transfer of license plate number 7 to his wife at the time.

Former state representative David W. Dumas puts it like this: "In England, you get a knighthood. Here, you get a low plate number." Low-number license plates were owned only by the powerful or connected until 1995, when Lincoln Almond became governor and instituted a state lottery system for low-number plates. So that solved

Not just a low number but doubled last digits. Clearly passed down through the family.

everything, right? Wrong. Scandals over low-number plates continued, to the point where current governor Donald Carcieri made fair distribution of license plates part of his campaign platform. But even the law couldn't stop Rhode Island's love for low-digit plates. In October 2005 two former Rhode Island judges ran off with their special judicial license plates, and ignored numerous requests from the state supreme court to return the plates.

My own family has been in Rhode Island for a few generations, and while we don't have any political connections to speak of, my parents are blessed with a very desirable license plate. But if you're a Rhode Islander, you now have a chance to get a good low-number plate yourself. Just enter your request on a 3-by-5 card and include your name, address, phone number, current registration number, and what type of plate you are requesting. Mail your request to Governor's Office, Office of Constituent Affairs, State House—Room 115, Providence, RI 02903, and you'll be entered in the fall when the governor announces the next lottery. Just be aware that a few thousand people will be competing for a few dozen plates.

From Russia, With Love

Quick, where's the only place in North America that you can see a former Soviet cruise missile submarine in all its glory? No, it isn't Moscow, Idaho. It's Collier Point Park in Providence, home to the Juliett-484, a 300-foot-long Russian submarine now converted into a museum. Yes, complete with giant red star, a soviet sub now sits in Providence, open for the world to walk through. And people are just Russian to get in.

Oddly enough, the people that brought the Juliett-484 to Providence were the folks from the USS *Saratoga* Museum Foundation, based around the USS *Saratoga*. Why is that odd? Well, back when it was in service, Russian submarines of the Juliett class tended to target U.S. Navy ships, especially the USS *Saratoga*. How would you feel if the peo-

Come one, come all, comerade, to the (red-) star attraction.

ple charged with taking care of you brought the person who had been trying to kill you into your own backyard? You'd probably think that the whole situation was sub-optimal.

Anyway, the Juliett-484 was built in a Gorky Russian shipyard in 1963 and launched in 1965. Nobody can say exactly what it did, because the mission logs are still a Russian secret. But we do know that the Juliett class of submarine is about as big as non-nuclear diesel submarines ever get, with a large buoyancy reserve and a double hull. They tended to target cities in the eastern United States, until the advent of ballistic missiles relegated the Juliett largely into a weapon against ships. The Juliett-484 was sold to a Finnish man named Jari Komulainen after the Cold War, who opened it as a restaurant. It was then borrowed in 2000 for the movie *K-19: The Widowmaker,* starring Harrison Ford, before being purchased by the USS *Saratoga* Museum Foundation in 2002.

Although the sub is called Juliett-484, that was apparently a ruse to hide its true name, which the foundation was told was K-81/B-81. But after scouring the sub and finding several logs and reports, it turns out that its name was K-77/B-77. This is why nobody plays submarine bingo. Anyway, the Juliett-484 is open for you to poke around in, and pretty soon they'll even be able to raise and lower the periscopes. So what does it take to get in? Just three tests of courage. First, you must wear shoes because sandals aren't allowed. Second, you must pass through a fake submarine hatch before boarding the actual submarine, just like an army drill. And third, you must face the admission fee. Thankfully, this is only a few bucks, which isn't too bad. The Russian Sub Museum is open on weekends; go to www.saratogamuseum.org or call (401) 521–3600 for more information.

Keep on Dunkin'

Rhode Islanders love their coffee and donuts. "So what?" you ask. "Doesn't every state love coffee and donuts?" Well, in a word, no. Or in six more precise words, not as much as Rhode Island. Perhaps because coffee milk is the state drink, Rhode Islanders have a love affair with coffee-flavored things that goes far beyond your typical coffee addict. In addition to (of course) drinking more coffee milk than any other state, Rhode Island also has the highest per capita consumption of coffee-flavored ice cream. And what about actual coffee? Well, Providence has more coffee and donut shops per capita than anywhere else in the country.

Dunkin' Donuts are so ubiquitous in Providence, you'd need a guidebook to find an area without one.

Still not convinced? Well, when it comes to coffee, Rhode Islanders tend to buy it at Dunkin' Donuts. There are more Dunkin' Donuts per square mile (and some have said per capita, though this is harder to verify) in Rhode Island than anywhere else in the world—and they keep building more. Could that be because Dunkin' Donuts is based in Rhode Island? Nope. Dunkin' Donuts is actually based in Massachusetts, but nobody likes them more than Rhode Island. There are 168 Dunkin' Donuts stores in Rhode Island for the million or so people there, in spite of the abundance of other coffee and donut shops in the state. But that's what Rhode Islanders want: coffee, coffee ice cream, and coffee milk. The three combined pretty much make a complete meal.

> *Though it's true that Rhode Island is small,*
> *We like donuts much more than you all.*
> *There are donuts to eat*
> *Every five hundred feet,*
> *And we'll likely add more by next fall.*

Monsters of Creativity

If you were to walk the streets around City Hall in Providence, you might see some of the most bizarre, grotesque, and wonderful creatures you've ever laid eyes on—and we're not just talking about the mayor. Because just across the street from City Hall lies the headquarters of Big Nazo. Though it may sound like a wing of the Mafia, Big Nazo is actually a group of performance artists, puppet masters, and musicians, led by the master puppet master Erminio Pinque. While words can hardly do justice to the experience of seeing the Big Nazo puppets out and about, Erminio says what they do is a combination of circus, science fiction, wrestling, vaudeville, and rock 'n' roll, all wrapped up in an alien bundle.

It all began as accidental street theater. "We didn't intend to become a street theater troupe," says Erminio. "We just wanted to do random fun performance art—anarchy with an unsuspecting public." He led a few fellow students at the Rhode Island School of Design—as well as some random local artists, performers, and musicians—in a grand scheme to subvert reality. In the giant creature costumes they crafted, they would appear at parties with a wild entourage, go out and wrestle, or simply run through public places where people would shop or eat. It was, in Erminio's words, "a guerrilla marketing campaign for nonsense, done by escapees from an art asylum."

But people saw the costumes and the reactions, and began approaching them with requests to do birthday parties and shows at schools. The street theater wasn't meant to be done for money, but serendipity dictated the career path. They did street theater in Italy, where they picked up the name Big Nazo (*nazo* is Italian for "nose"). They refined their technique in Providence, Boston, and New York, becoming very serious about improving their craft. Eventually they were asked to attend an international street performance festival, in

Just a few characters from Big Nazo's extensive cast. Just goes to show, clothes make the man.

spite of the fact that they weren't even an official troupe. They won third prize.

The group usually consists of just six to eleven people, but another few dozen can be called upon when needed (and after all, when *don't* you need a few dozen crazy creatures running around?). Though working with Big Nazo requires many skills, from acting and improvisation to art-making, they always seem to have enough collaborators. Erminio never really seeks people out for these positions, they just show up.

The Big Nazo storefront studio is right in the middle of Providence, with their window of crazy monsters and puppets a shining beacon of inspired madness amid an otherwise ordinary day. It's no surprise that he gets a lot of walk-in visitors. People come in to ask about getting hired, or just to dress up and take pictures. Erminio teaches a course at RISD called Creature Creation, and he still occasionally gets people coming in to say, "I remember you from when I was in fifth grade. Your creatures ate my principal."

And the creatures continue to amaze. Quasi, a balding puppet I remember from when I was young, still leads the band. They have a menagerie of literally hundreds of creatures, ranging from monsters that are mostly food to monsters that are mostly mouth. They often perform less as entertainers and more as rowdy guests, humorously improvising while simply being the characters in real time. And as characters go, they are probably the strangest ones you will ever see in your entire life.

If you're walking through Providence, you can find the Big Nazo Lab on the corner of Fulton and Eddy Streets, just across from City Hall. Look for the giant bizarre monsters in the window. If you're not in Providence, you can find more information about Big Nazo on their Web site, www.bignazo.com.

Trafficking in Entertainment

Ever since Judge Wapner presided over *The People's Court,* people have had a fascination with watching actual court cases on television. And while few Rhode Islanders will get a chance to have Judge Judy decide their case in front of a television audience, a surprisingly large number of them will be judged on TV by Chief Municipal Court Judge Frank Caprio.

Judge Caprio is the host, star, and judge of the Rhode Island television series *Caught in Providence*. Each week, ten cases in Providence Municipal Court are put on the air, so all of the state can see what really goes on in traffic court. You might think this sounds like a terrible idea for a TV show, but they'll put anything on public access. A funny thing happened, though: The show got so popular that it was picked up by the local ABC affiliate. It has remained on ABC-6 for a number of years, and its popularity can probably be attributed to two main factors.

First, Rhode Island is a small state, small enough that if you've lived there your whole life, the chances of your knowing one of the ten people being tried on any given episode are actually fairly decent. And few things are as gratifying as seeing the guy who cut in front of you at the bank line failing to weasel his way out of a ticket. Actually, watching people fail to weasel out of tickets is generally entertaining, which is the other reason the show has stayed on the air. People have attempted to cite every conceivable reason why they shouldn't have to pay, including one woman who said she didn't know she was speeding because her shoes were too tight.

"You could never script the excuses that are here before this court," says Judge Caprio. Perhaps that's what prompted him to become the driving force behind *Caught in Providence*.

And if you're a night owl, you can watch it early in the morning on ABC-6.

Come Hell and High Water

In the middle of the twentieth century, Rhode Island was hit by a pair of hurricanes that caused some serious flooding. First, in 1938 came the Great New England Hurricane. These winds came up from Florida and caught everyone in New England—especially everyone in Rhode Island—completely by surprise. Why surprise? Well, prior to that, there hadn't been a big hurricane in Rhode Island since 1815. Heck, some people didn't even know what a hurricane was. But the 120-miles-per-hour winds came right at the time of high tide, causing waters to rise 13 feet above normal and doing $100 million in property damage just in Rhode Island.

Then in 1954 Hurricane Carol had winds of 100 mph and came to wreak havoc once again in the form of flooding throughout Providence.

Anyone who was alive during either of these hurricanes and floods no doubt remembers the waters. A few years ago the *Providence Journal* even ran a fifty-year anniversary story about the flood of 1954. But the best way to understand how high the floodwaters came is to visit Providence today, where two plaques on the side of the Amica Building at 10 Weybosset Street in the middle of the city can give you a real sense of history.

The top plaque reads DURING THE HURRICANE AND FLOOD OF SEPTEMBER 21, 1938, THE WATERS ROSE TO THIS LEVEL. The bottom plaque reads DURING THE HURRICANE AND FLOOD OF AUGUST 31, 1954, THE WATERS ROSE TO THIS LEVEL. And the subtext reads "We sell insurance, and maybe you should buy some, because you never know what will happen."

Your hair might have stayed dry in the 1954 flood, but the 1938 floodwaters rose higher.

Date with Density

Imagine that you are a new student at Brown University, and some of your new buddies have just set you up on a blind date for 8:00 tonight. All you have to do is go to the corner of Prospect and Waterman, two of the main streets on the Brown campus, and this beautiful girl named Carrie Tower will meet you there. So you take a quick shower, shave, and head over to the corner of the two streets, where you wait for this girl to show up. Half an hour later, you start to wonder if you're being stood up, so in desperation you ask a passerby if they have seen Carrie Tower around. They point upwards, and as you follow their hand, you suddenly realize you've been pranked.

She's built like a brick house. And, well . . .

Carrie Tower is a 95-foot-high redbrick edifice that was built in 1904 as a gift from Paul Bajnotti of Turin, Italy. He had it erected as a memorial to his wife, who was the granddaughter of Nicholas Brown, who in turn was the man that Brown University was named for. The tower has elaborately carved stonework, four clock faces, the inscription LOVE IS STRONG AS DEATH on the bottom—and a history of being used for pranks. The Blind Date with Carrie Tower gag was always a favorite to pull on incoming students back in the day, but sometimes the pranks were more ambitious. In 1950 hats belonging to the corporation that governs Brown University were stolen and placed atop Carrie Tower. To focus attention on the hats, the pranksters also removed a few parts from the clock inside the tower so it stopped running correctly.

Sadly, both the blind date prank and the stuff-atop-the-tower gag seem to have fallen out of popularity. But hopefully the new generation of Brown students will find some entertaining pranks to make with the tower and will Carrie on the tradition.

Turk-y

If you walk through the middle of Providence, you will likely pass West-minster and Weybosset Streets. And if you walk to the intersection of the two (which is V-shaped, because they are non-perpendicular streets), you will notice a giant head staring at you. No, it's not your hydroencephalic friend. The big head is that of a Turk. But don't worry, he won't attack you, because he's stoned. The Turk's head is made of granite, and it stands proudly at the rounded front of the Turk's Head Build-ing, which was designed in 1913 and built by the Brown Land Co.

It's always nice to know someone's watching over you.

As you might have guessed, the Turk's Head Building was named after a Turk's head. As you might not have guessed, it was not named after the current stone head. In the mid-eighteenth century, a man named Jacob Whitman had a house on that site with a carving of a Turk's head on his porch. This was in the days when carved images served as signs, and with images more common than street names, the corner was just called "Turk's Head." Some say the head was the figure-head from a ship called the *Sultan,* but whatever the case, the current stone head is there to give a nod to the building's history.

The impressive Turk's Head Building is sixteen stories high and was built upon a base of sturdy columns. This was a newish development in construction back in the early twentieth century when the building was erected, but like the Turk's Head itself, today it's just something we all take for granite.

Hearty Vegetation

Roger Williams was the man who founded Rhode Island, and he did so because religious freedom was near to his heart. After he died, how-ever, what was near to his heart was a tree. Actually, *near* doesn't quite do it justice. A better word might be *in*.

Yes, *in*. Roger Williams was buried in 1684 in his own backyard. In 1860 his remains were dug up to be moved to a family crypt in the North Burial Ground, but what they found was very surprising: The cof-fin was in scraps and pieces, and the apple tree that was next to his grave had grown down through the coffin into Roger Williams himself. The roots of the tree had grown right through the spot where his head would have rested, and then into his chest. The apple tree had con-sumed the founder of Rhode Island, essentially using him as fertilizer. It

can be said, in more ways than one, he is truly part of what made this land what it is.

The few bits of bones that could be salvaged were reburied, eventually to be moved once again in 1936 to their current location on Prospect Hill. But far more interesting is the tree root itself, which to some degree even took the shape of Roger Williams. This root was saved, and is currently guarded by the Rhode Island Historical Society. They do not, alas, have it on display, but it remains in their care at the John Brown House Museum at 52 Power Street (401–273–7507). While random visitors are not permitted to view the root, perhaps you can convince the Historical Society that you are a special case.

We'll be rooting for you.

King of the Hill

Federal Hill is Providence's Italian district. Yes, an even more Italian district than the rest of Providence, which says something. And on Federal Hill, restaurants come and go as fast as the seasons. But one of the few restaurants to endure for decades is the favored pizza parlor of the Providence people: Caserta Pizzeria.

The restaurant has been at the same spot for more than fifty years, and for the last two decades has been owned by the Campagnone family. Owner John Campagnone says that the secret of his success is simplicity. Instead of the vast menus of most modern pizza places, Caserta Pizzeria offers all of five toppings: cheese, pepperoni, mushrooms, olives, and anchovies. Those are your choices for a pizza, end of story. And simplicity works, because Caserta's is well-known throughout Rhode Island, though it's hard to say whether they are more famous for their pizza or the Wimpy Skippy.

The Wimpy Skippy, as you probably already know if you live in Providence, is a spinach pie filled with pepperoni and cheese. It was named by the previous owners for a pair of their friends (nicknamed, surprisingly enough, Wimpy and Skippy) who used to eat there all the time. It costs a little more than three bucks, and while it sounds weird, tastes delicious. People come from across the state just to get them. And you can eat them with your hands.

That's important, because Caserta's does not have any silverware, or plasticware, or anything of the sort. We did mention that the owner is a big fan of simplicity, right? "We have pizza and pizza-related products," says Campagnone. "We don't have pasta, we don't have salads, and we don't have sandwiches." Also, they don't have freezers, so they make all their food fresh. And they have no credit card machine, so bring cash. Pretty much what they've got is pizza with five toppings, sausage

Home of the Wimpy Skippy, and if you're unadventurous, pizza.

calzones, and the Wimpy Skippy. That's it. But thankfully, it's tasty enough to make it well worth your while. You'll find Caserta Pizzeria (401–621–3618) at 121 Spruce Street.

The Jig Is Up

Some people think that directing traffic is the most boring thing in the world. But people who have seen Officer Tony LePore, aka "The Dancing Cop," often think that few things are more exciting than directing traffic. Because the Dancing Cop, as you might expect, dances and madly gesticulates in order to tell the cars when to go. His white-gloved hands spin in circles and curve in waves just like the rest of his body, to the delight of Rhode Islanders since 1984.

Tony LePore became Officer LePore in the early 1970s when he joined the Providence Police Department. After nine years on night duty and two medals of valor, he switched to day duty, which included directing traffic at the corner of Dorrance and Westminster Streets. Two years of normal traffic direction quickly proved boring, so one day in 1984, Officer LePore decided to add a little pizzazz with some elaborate hand movements and spinning. "The little boy in me just came out," says LePore, who had been a bit of a class clown in his youth.

He quickly won statewide fame, and since public reaction was so positive, his bosses had no problem with it. LePore continued adding more moves to his traffic-directing repertoire until he retired in 1988. But the public wanted more dancin' to the beat, on the beat, and newspapers began asking, whatever happened to the Dancing Cop? Finally, in the early 1990s, Providence mayor Buddy Cianci asked LePore if he would come back and direct traffic during the holiday season. LePore agreed, was re-sworn in as a part-time officer, and directed traffic at a few intersections across Providence in the way that only he can. Naturally, the public was thrilled.

This tradition has continued every year since then, with Officer LePore's dancing directions becoming so popular that he has received much national and even some international media attention. What's the secret to his success? Partially his fitness routine of lifting weights and running 4 miles a few times a week, and partially just good knee pads, because otherwise the John Travolta routine would be extremely painful.

So if you're driving through Providence in December and you see a police officer directing traffic with a pirouette, you'll know it's none other than the Dancing Cop.

Catch-22

What's your favorite number? And how much do you really like it? Probably not as much as the man whose legal name is Love 22. He really, really, really likes the number 22. Really. And that's why three decades ago, he changed his name from Lawrence Wagner to Love 22. Well, that's not the only reason. In fact, he gave the judge in Providence precisely 22 reasons why he should have his name legally changed. For example, in college at the University of Rhode Island, his football jersey was number 22, as was the address of his fraternity house.

As you'd expect from someone with his name, Love 22 is a numerologist. He believes that a lot can be learned about a person using their birthday and name and running the numbers. He has his own letter-value chart where A=1, B=2, and on through I=9, which then restarts with J=1, and so on. Using this chart to assign a value to each letter, Love 22 puts quotation marks around any phrase or word whose values add up to 22; for example, "LOVE-2-2" [L=3, O=6, V=4, E=5, and

3+6+4+5+2+2=22]. Note that the reason I used brackets instead of parentheses there is because Love 22 also uses parentheses around phrases containing exactly 22 letters.

The phrase (UNITED STATES GOVERNMENT) has 22 letters, which may be the reason why Love 22 has had such an interesting political career. He has run for governor of Rhode Island as an independent candidate for many years, though he has not yet won. He is also the country's longest-running write-in candidate for president, perhaps inspired by the 22-ness of the phrase (A PRESIDENTIAL CANDIDATE). His platform, unsurprisingly, consists of 22 planks.

So how does he fund all these campaigns? With "$22 BILLS" of course. He prints up $22 bills which include his letter-value chart and his own smiling face dressed as Uncle Sam. Although the bills are quite obviously not valid currency, they have been cashed hundreds of times. He has even been brought in twice on counterfeiting charges in connection with his $22 bills, but the judge ruled in his favor both times.

At the moment, Love 22 lives in Florida, but everyone knows him as a (TRUE CRAZY RHODE ISLANDER). For more 22-laden text than you can shake a stick at, visit his Web site at www.love22.com.

A Bury Good Library

Brown University may be famous for its elite Ivy League status and lack of required curriculum, but their library collection is what you should really be dying to see. John Hay was one of Abraham Lincoln's secretaries and an alumnus of Brown University. The John Hay Library (20 Prospect Street; 401–863–3723) was named for him, and thanks to various donations by people with names like Rockefeller, holds a very large collection of Lincoln memorabilia. This collection features copies of two casts taken of Lincoln's face, five years apart. Some have mistaken the later cast as a death mask due to his sad and peaceful expression, but it was taken while he was alive.

As for death, there are some books you can check out. Well, maybe you can't literally check them out, but you should definitely check them out. Three books in the John Hay Library are wrapped in human skin (not Lincoln's skin), including an anatomy textbook. I think it's worth a look, but if you disagree, no skin off my back.

Brown University also owns the Annmary Brown Memorial (21 Brown Street; 401–863–2942), which can best be described as a combination museum and mausoleum. This tomb hosts a variety of paintings, swords, relics, and the late General Rush Hawkins and his wife, who are buried in a crypt towards the end of the building. Most of the books from the mausoleum have been transferred to the John Hay Library, but if you want to visit General and Mrs. Hawkins, just drop by any summer afternoon during the week.

A Well-Knocked Dorr

Thomas Wilson Dorr was a governor in Rhode Island. However, Dorr was never the official governor of Rhode Island, and was considered entirely illegitimate by the ruling government at the time. We like him anyway. In 1841 only land-owning white men were eligible for the vote in Rhode Island, which excluded well over half of the free white male population. Dorr and his followers felt that constitutionally, the vote should be given to all free white males, as it was in every other state. But Rhode Island loves to be different, and the General Assembly at the time was resistant to change.

Dorr and friends held a convention in 1841, which drafted "The People's Constitution." This constitution, appropriately, extended the vote to the people. The slight flaw with this was that the Rhode Island General Assembly didn't recognize said constitution, and thus also didn't recognize the voting rights of 60 percent of the populace. So it was in 1842 that Thomas Wilson Dorr was elected governor of the people, and Samuel Ward King was reelected official governor of Rhode Island. As you might suspect, this caused a bit of friction.

Dorr's Rebellion began when Dorr and friends (which would make a great TV show) decided to march on the state arsenal in Providence and demand its surrender. King's government did not surrender, but instead sent in the state militia. Dorr's erstwhile friends all ran away to avoid being killed, and Dorr himself fled into exile. Upon returning, he was put on trial for treason against Rhode Island (which is odd, because treason can only be against a country, not a chartered local government). Dorr never apologized, insisting his actions had all been justified by the people's will. He was given a life sentence of solitary confinement and hard labor, of which he served one year before being released due to a combination of poor health and public outrage.

Though Dorr himself may have lost, his struggle for the people's freedom was successful and resulted in an extension of the vote in Rhode Island. And to this day, you can vote in Rhode Island even if you don't own land. Dorr's current land, meanwhile, is at Swan Point Cemetery in Providence.

Luck of the Italian

The Italians and the Irish are not known for their love for each other. So it should perhaps come as no surprise that the large Italian population of Rhode Island (second only to Connecticut, percentage-wise) was not enthusiastic about celebrating St. Patrick's Day. Conveniently, there's an Italian holiday just two days later called St. Joseph's Day, which is a big

Federal Hill: more Italian than Italy itself.

event for all of Rhode Island. For people in Italy, St. Joseph's Day is about the Nazarene carpenter St. Joseph delivering them from famine, celebrated by putting special foods, flowers, and festive statues on the three-step St. Joseph's Altar. For Rhode Islanders, St. Joseph's Day is largely about zeppole.

Zeppole is, to be fair, one of the special foods that are generally placed on the altar in Italy. But in Rhode Island, it's the ubiquitous pastry treat that is available all over the state every St. Joseph's Day. Zeppole look vaguely like a filled donut but are generally Italian bread dough that has been fried (or occasionally baked) and filled with custard or cannoli cream. Older recipes call for ricotta cheese and cinnamon, or even just honey, but the modern recipe zeppole are the ones that fill the bakeries of Rhode Island every March 19. What better way to celebrate an end to famine than to wolf down a few specially made holiday pastries?

Despite St. Joseph's Day's vast popularity in Rhode Island, many states seem not to celebrate the holiday at all. Perhaps this is why Rhode Islanders away from home get zeppole cravings in March. But bakeries on Federal Hill (Rhode Island's Little Italy) make such good zeppole that native Italians have talked about missing the zeppole of Rhode Island. So next March 19, wish everyone you see a happy St. Joseph's Day. And if you're near Rhode Island, stop in for some zeppole. It's a holiday food you *do-nut* want to miss.

A Storied Past

The first thing you may notice when you look at Len Cabral is his long hair. But the great experience comes when you start listening to Len, because he is one of Providence's—and Rhode Island's—most beloved storytellers. In an age where most children are spoon-fed stories of mush through television, Len Cabral is out serving gourmet banquets of engrossing stories to children all over the state (and country, and world).

I may be slightly biased because I spent my childhood listening to his stories of the African trickster-spider Anansi. (He was one of my role models—not Len, the spider.) But Len has been telling stories even longer than that, ever since working at a day-care center in Providence in the early 1970s. "I was in charge of fifteen five-year olds," says Len. "That will make you a storyteller."

So tell stories he did, using them as a teaching tool before joining a theater company and eventually touring. He has now been a profes-sional storyteller for more than thirty years, and has come to an under-standing of what makes stories work. "A good story is one that engages the listeners," Len explains, "that connects with people and that people can connect with." He also likes to make the listener go "Aha!"

From his bag of tempting tales, Len refuses to name a favorite, saying that they all are his favorite. "You have to love them all to tell them right," he says. In addition to his family of stories, he also loves his family of two daughters, a wife, two caring parents, and a strong influence from his Cape Verdean grandmother. As the great-grandson of a Cape Verdean whaler, Len's ancestry is important to him, and that's no tall tale.

If you do want to hear some tall tales, though, visit his Web site at www.lencabral.com to find out when he will next be performing near you.

Have Trademark Infringement, Will Travel

You've probably never heard of Victor DeCosta of Providence, but if you watched television in the 1950s and 1960s, you're probably more familiar with him than you realize.

DeCosta was a cowboy who used to dress in black and hand out cards with a picture of a chess knight that said "Have Gun, Will Travel." He also had the nickname of *Paladin*, ever since an Italian man at a horse show stood up and called him paladino. This bears a non-trivial resemblance to the CBS television show called *Have Gun—Will Travel*, which starred a cowboy dressed in black named Paladin, who handed out business cards with a chess knight that said "Have Gun, Will Travel."

See the similarities? What's more, the Paladin character on CBS even looked like DeCosta. DeCosta filed a trademark infringement suit against CBS, but his victories were continually appealed. It took decades before he finally managed to get a judgment in his favor in 1991 for roughly $3 million. Sadly, he never managed to collect even this, and died in 1993. But while almost nobody remembers his name, the legend of Paladin will certainly live on forever.

PROVIDENCE COUNTY

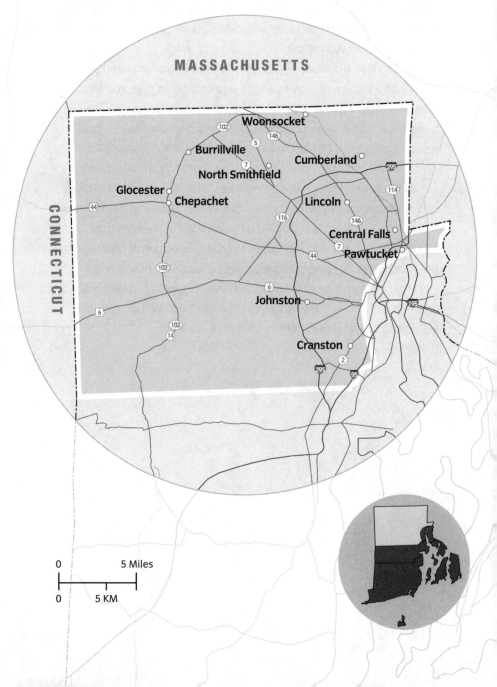

MASSACHUSETTS

CONNECTICUT

Woonsocket

Burrillville

North Smithfield

Cumberland

Glocester
Chepachet

Lincoln

Central Falls

Pawtucket

Johnston

Cranston

0   5 Miles

0   5 KM

PROVIDENCE COUNTY

Pullet Surprise

Burrillville

The Blackstone River Valley is famous for family–style chicken, and no restaurant in the valley is as well-known as Wright's Farm. This restaurant, managed by Frank Galleshaw III, serves up all the chicken you can eat, along with salad, pasta, french fries, and rolls. Family–style chicken has been a local favorite since the 1930s, so much so that most weddings in northern Rhode Island have chicken family–style on the menu. But why, you ask, is Wright's Farm not owned by Wright?

Well, chicken supplier Gene Wright began doing outdoor barbecues in the 1950s, and his popularity led him to open the Wright's Farm Restaurant in 1954. The restaurant was purchased by Frank Galleshaw Jr. in 1972, already so popular that despite seating 400 people at once, there were still twenty-minute wait times. Galleshaw Jr. decided to add a room every few years to increase capacity, boasting that the main reason people came to Burrillville was to come to Wright's Farm. When Frank Galleshaw Jr. died in 2000, his son Frank Galleshaw III took over, and the restaurant today has six dining rooms, four full bars, and four kitchens commanding seventy-five ovens. Wright's Farm goes through seven tons of chicken and six tons of french fries every week, and can serve 1,000 people at once—more than any other restaurant in the state.

In spite of this, it's still often crowded, so showing up early is recommended. The restaurant is in the middle of nowhere, and there aren't really many signs for it, but Rhode Islanders always manage to find their way there. After fifty years of business, says Galleshaw, the reputation speaks for itself. "People know what to expect. You're guaranteed to get a great meal, in a family atmosphere." And he's not kidding about the family atmosphere. The family–style chicken attracts many families. And many families work for Galleshaw—some of the servers have parents who had worked at Wright's Farm, and some of *their* parents also worked at Wright's. And, of course, the Galleshaw family runs the whole operation.

How can you not buy chicken from this man?

In addition to the Wright's Farm Restaurant that Frank oversees, his wife and sister manage the 4,000-square-foot gift shop on the premises. His sister's husband is in charge of their food products division, distributing Wright's Farm products to hundreds of stores across New England. You might say Galleshaw's whole family is in chicken. Of course, if family–style chicken doesn't appeal to you, you can still go to Wright's Farm and enjoy all-you-can-eat french fries, salad, macaroni, bread, and a huge steak, but everyone else will look at you funny as they eat their chicken.

Wright's Farm Restaurant is located at 84 Inman Road, Burrillville. For more information call (401) 769–2856 or visit www.wrightsfarm.com.

Cuckoo for Cocoa Dust
Central Falls

Nowadays, the place in America known for chocolate is Hershey, Pennsylvania. But a few hundred years ago, Central Falls was the big chocolate-processing place. Back in 1780 Sylvanus Brown built a dam across the Blackstone River, and thus was founded a mill that was known as the Chocolate Mill. The Chocolate Mill didn't just make chocolate, it also made tools. But tools are boring, and you can't eat them. More importantly, many mills made tools, but chocolate was one of the first luxury items being produced in the area. The mill ground cacao beans into cocoa, because apparently grinding things swaps their vowels.

Regardless, having a chocolate mill was so exciting that the whole area became known as Chocolateville. A man named Wheat was the big manufacturer of chocolate at the time, probably surprising everyone who thought he'd be grinding flour, not cocoa. Chocolateville was a hopping town, and the location right on the river meant that a lot of mills sprung up there—so many, in fact, that it became the country's most densely populated city. Most historians argue that the mills are what brought the people, but chocolate has its own siren song. The Chocolate Mill continued crushing cacao beans in the name of Chocolateville until the 1820s, when the name was changed to Central Falls.

But Chocolateville remembers its history. Now, nearly two centuries later, Garrison Confections, a gourmet chocolate manufacturer, is moving their factory from Providence to Central Falls. The factory lets them take tons of processed chocolate and turn it into many gourmet chocolates. But that isn't thinking big enough for Andrew Shotts, award-winning chocolatier and owner of Garrison Confections. He plans to build a huge factory for processing raw cacao beans into cocoa, just like the Chocolate Mill of days gone by.

If the factory gets built, passersby will be able to peer in the windows at giant vats of chocolate, as the smells from the factory tempt them to go satisfy their sweet tooth. With the possibility of factory tours and a highly increased public profile, it appears that Central Falls may soon be Chocolateville once again.

The Learned Elephant
Chepachet

Were you to visit Chepachet, you might notice a perplexing plethora of pachyderm pieces for purchase. This is all due to the tale of one poor elephant named Little Bett. Little Bett was a celebrity elephant who toured America in the 1820s and was owned by a man named Hachaliah Bailey. If the name Bailey sounds familiar, that's because his family would go on to become a tremendous force in the circus world, and eventually form part of the Barnum & Bailey Circus (the Bailey part, to be precise).

What do you get when you cross a potato and an elephant? This.

Anyway, Hachaliah Bailey was touring with his elephant Little Bett, who was quite a draw. Most animals that toured the country were shown in large menageries, but elephants had star power. Bailey had previously toured with an elephant named Old Bett, who met with an unfortunate end in a Maine field. Bailey had been walking Old Bett into town on a Sunday, but they crossed paths with a fundamentalist farmer. The man apparently took exception to the idea that people might pay money to see this strange beast for entertainment, especially on a holy Sunday, and shot Old Bett, killing her. You could say that Bailey had lost a Bett.

Soon after, Bailey acquired Little Bett (whom he named after Old Bett) and began touring with her. As an added draw, not only was Little Bett still one of the first few elephants to tour the country, but she was also the first elephant to be trained to do tricks. Before Little Bett, people came to gape at the mere fact that elephants existed. Little Bett was much cooler, and could balance on any two legs, carry people around with her trunk, and uncork and drink bottles. She was called "The Learned Elephant," and Bailey successfully toured with her nationwide, including Chepachet in 1822 and again in 1826.

There once was an elephant, Bett,
Who was killed, which the townsfolk regret.
If you go walk around
Then you'll see that the town,
Like an elephant, doesn't forget.

But 1826 was to be Little Bett's last hurrah. Once again, Bailey's prize elephant would be shot and killed. A group of young men cornered Little Bett on the Chepachet Bridge, leveled their muskets at her, and fired. Some say that the men had tried to see Little Bett without paying earlier that day, and this was their revenge. Others say that the local Masonic Order was suspiciously quiet about the whole affair, especially given their connection to some of the shooters. Stories have even morphed to the point where some say Bailey was alongside her when she was heartlessly gunned down, and still others claim the elephant had escaped and was shot for that reason. But whatever the reasons, Little Bett died on May 25, 1826.

And Chepachet remembers. The bridge was quickly renamed Elephant Bridge, and though the original wooden structure was washed away in 1867, some people still call the Chepachet Bridge the Elephant Bridge today. On the 150th anniversary of Little Bett's death, the Rhode Island General Assembly proclaimed May 25, 1976, as Elephant Day, and a ceremony took place wherein a Little Bett commemorative plaque was placed on Elephant Bridge, where smaller ceremonies are still held annually. And the surrounding shops, perhaps by way of atonement, tend to have lots of elephant-themed items.

If you want to visit the Elephant Bridge, and the site of Little Bett's death, just take Route 44 into Chepachet and look for the bridge with the bronze plaque. Just don't forget to pack your trunk.

Ye Olde Shoppe
Chepachet

Stores love to pretend that they're old-timey. These days, it seems like every small town has a shop that throws together some bric-a-brac, sticks an extra letter or two at the end of a word (the e is quite popular), and calls itself an "Old-Fashioned Shoppe." Well, they're all imposters, mountebanks, hooligans, and charlatans—most of them, anyway. If you want the real deal, you'll come to Brown & Hopkins Country Store in Chepachet. Brown & Hopkins is the America's oldest country store in continuous operation, having been running nonstop since 1809. (Well, mostly nonstop. I mean, they do close at night and for holidays and so forth.)

As you might expect, however, the store has changed hands quite a few times during the intervening years. Originally built in 1799, the building was first put to use as a general store by Ira Evans, who bought it in 1809. It was in 1921 that the store was purchased by the dynamic duo of James Brown and William Hopkins. And no, it wasn't *that* James Brown. Brown and Hopkins ran the store until 1964, when they left but the name stayed. The current owners, Liz and Scott McIntyre, bought the store in 2004. Thankfully, they didn't change the name to McIntyre & McIntyre Country Store, because that doesn't sound as good.

A name that has been around a lot longer than you have.

In addition to the name, many other things have stayed the same as well. Brown & Hopkins is still in that same building built back in the eighteenth century, complete with beamed ceiling and wooden floors. Heck, even the potbelly stove is still there, though it doesn't run anymore. And the goods, while not entirely the same, do include a lot of throwback items, like homemade jams and primitive country home accessories. From reproduction furniture to period lighting, they may have bric-a-brac, but it's authentic country bric-a-brac.

Perhaps most importantly, especially for anyone with a sweet tooth, Brown & Hopkins continues the fine tradition of the oversize penny candy display. Where else can you get something to eat for a penny? Sure, you'll likely spend more than a few pennies for most items, especially if you want treats like rock candy. But that's a small price to pay for a caramel chew from America's oldest continuously operating country store. Because as that caramel gets stuck in your teeth, you can ask yourself, "I wonder if this one is leftover from 1809?"

The Brown & Hopkins Country Store is located at 1179 Putnam Pike in Chepachet. You can call (401) 568–4830 for more information.

Parade of Horribles

Chepachet

When people refer to a "parade of horribles," they usually mean a slippery slope argument about all the horrible things that could happen. But usually, those people aren't in Chepachet. Because Chepachet plays host each year to an actual parade of horribles on the Fourth of July, as many despicable things wind their way down the street. Yes, the Ancients and Horribles parade is quite real, and appropriately, both ancient and horrible.

It all began back in 1927, when the first Ancients and Horribles parade was held. Some say that the name was invented as a mockery of an old Boston organization called the Ancients and Honorables. Others say that it's a more straightforward combination of two early twentieth-century events: an ancient parade on wheels pulled by a trolley when the town first got a trolley line, and a horribles parade of men costumed in various Halloweenish garb. But whatever the origin of the name, the Ancients and Horribles parade has continued to grace the Main Street of Chepachet for many decades, in a bizarre combination of political roast, Halloween pageant, and patriotic parade.

On the one hand, you've got the Ancients: the smartly dressed marching bands, the honorable color guards, patriotic floats honoring the military or the country's founding fathers, and various other people all paying homage to the Fourth of July. But much more interesting are the Horribles, which mock everything from local issues to national scandals.

What's the secret to getting really zany floats? A complete lack of restrictions on entry! Anyone at all can participate in the parade, which leads to some fairly irreverent floats and paraders that would surely be stopped at any other parade. Like the man dressed as Patrick Kennedy

The Ancients and Horribles parade attracts many men and women. And combinations of both.

driving a green cardboard car, mocking the young Kennedy's crash into a barricade on Capitol Hill. Or better yet, the float "Dick Cheney's Hunting Party," lampooning the vice president for shooting a lawyer in the face while quail hunting. Now that's what I call a parade! Could anything possibly stop such a wonderful tradition?

Actually, yes. Waking up early could stop it, and almost did. For more than seventy-five years, the parade was held in the late afternoon. But in 2004 the police department asked that the parade start in the morning to discourage public alcohol consumption. The turnout was . . . well, horrible. Almost nobody showed up to march in the parade. The 11:00 A.M. starting time was repeated in 2005, and the pathetic lack of attendance was also repeated. But never let it be said that the town council can't learn from experience. For the 2006 parade, they reverted to the ancient late afternoon start time and began at 4:00 P.M. And once again, the crowds showed up, and all was well.

If you want more information about the parade, you can contact chairperson Connie Leathers at (401) 864–8239. But be warned: Since anyone can march in the parade, even the parade committee has no idea how many participants they will have until soon before it begins. Still, in addition to the surrounding activities like clowns and face painting, you can count on marching bands, military units, and various floats that are bound to make you smile. Just so long as they don't hold it in the morning.

Vampire Hunter
Cranston

Most vampire hunters only exist in movies or on TV. But Cranston's Michael Bell has spent many years hunting vampires all over New England. Granted, he doesn't come across many living vampires these days, but as one of New England's premier folklore experts, he tracks their stories and histories very carefully.

Michael has an MA in Folklore and Mythology and a PhD in Folklore, so his schooling isn't just a myth. But his biggest attraction to folklore was his biggest attraction— his wife. She was teaching high school English and using folklore to interest her students in reading, which had caused Michael to shift his focus. They've now been married for more than forty years, and while his wife has long since changed careers, Michael has stayed with the folklore.

A vampire hunter in repose. He knows that you're just food for the dead.

In fact, when the Rhode Island Historical Society needs to know something about folklore, they tend to turn to Michael Bell. He has spearheaded a number of programs to help preserve Rhode Island's folklore, with help from other similarly interested people, and has a large collection of pictures and recordings which he plans to make into a public archive.

Meanwhile, Michael has collected all of the vampire stories he has heard into a volume called *Food for the Dead: On the Trail of New England's Vampires*. The title comes from an old quote about vampires killing people without leaving their graves, such that the living become food for the dead. The book includes his favorite tales, such as the story of famed Rhode Island vampire Mercy Brown, including a report that he heard from someone who heard it from an eyewitness.

Rhode Island is a small enough state that I doubt any vampires could remain anonymous here for long. But if there were any vampires about, be confident that Michael Bell is tracking them down.

Lawn Order
Cranston

Christmas is a time for decorated trees, reindeer, and Santas. Then again, if you're Joe Moretti, those decorations might include Martha Stewart or Paris Hilton. Because Joe is not really what you'd call a traditionalist.

Well, that's not quite fair. Christmas decorations are a tradition for him, as he's been doing them for three decades, ever since he was nine years old. It's just that his traditions are slightly . . . different. He may have had reindeer, but they were pink. He earned money for his displays by selling fruit out of a baby carriage, and people began eagerly anticipating his yearly displays.

Joe began adding celebrities to his displays, and became infamous in 1988 with a Liberace–themed one. He won a $1,000 first prize for best decoration in Cranston, and used the money to finance the following year's display. He won again, used the prize for the next year, and kept his rule over Yule running for half a decade.

Most people look forward to his yearly displays, and his Paris Hilton one in 2005 certainly turned many heads. Joe doesn't mean to offend anyone, and says anyone who doesn't like it can just drive by and not look.

Seems unlikely, though, given that most cars passing his house near Christmas slow down or stop altogether to appreciate the visual holiday feast he provides. Normal things just "didn't rock my world," says Joe, and his passion for creativity inspired him to decorate with some wonderfully bizarre flair. (This is also why he has an interior design business.)

Joe Moretti's 2006 tribute to Oprah.

So what does he have in store for Christmas this year? Well, he already knows, but he's not telling, because he wants it to be a surprise. Seeing people's smiles and wide eyes as they stop on the road is his biggest reward, so if you're in Cranston around Christmastime, go see what Joe has in store.

Big Head, Big Ideas

Cranston

Despite being the man behind Big Head Studio, Scott Bonelli's cranium is of a fairly average size—but what's in that cranium is probably dangerous. Bonelli was in theater design for many years, ever since he was sixteen. He kept building props and tried to master as many trades as possible. After sixteen years of building theater props, he amassed plenty of tradesmanship, but his breakthrough came when famed designer Michael McGarty asked him to build a gigantic fiberglass head. Originally it was just planned as a model, but it was decided that a 14-foot head needed to be built, and Bonelli won the bid. The gigantic foam sculpture cost roughly $10,000, was covered in nine gallons of liquid latex, and towered over the production it was used for. In case you're curious, it was named Dave.

Anyway, that 14-foot behemoth noggin is the reason for the name Big Head Studio. But perhaps unsurprisingly, most of Bonelli's projects do not involve building humongous heads. Some of them involve very tiny skulls instead, such as the Siamese twin skull he crafted for use in sideshows. In fact, Bonelli produces a number of sideshow artifacts that combine the real and the fake, to the point where it's hard to tell where one ends and the other begins. His conjoined baby piglet fetuses in a jar are real piglet fetuses, but may not have started conjoined. The necklace on display from the Fugawe tribe is made from real pieces of bone, but the Fugawe tribe is just an old joke. His human skullcaps and mercury-preserved human hands may have fake histories, but the pieces are real.

So, people come to Big Head Studio for theater props, and for sideshow oddities. In spite of his tiny basement in his Cranston house, he makes things of any size. He dreams of opening his own sideshow curiosities tent, where people try to figure out what's real. Even experts are fooled by some of his work, and Penn & Teller own some of his creations. Still, Big Head Studio isn't all sideshow props. After covering a 14-foot head in gallons of liquid latex, Bonelli found he preferred painting smaller and more animate canvases, so now paints live bodies on Thursday nights. To think, when most artists say they're going to paint a nude model, they mean something different. He also creates various adult toys, but we're not going to write about that because my mom's reading this book. Hi, Mom!

Whether you want more information about painting pretty things, viewing sideshow grotesqueries, or building colossal braincases, you can reach Scott Bonelli at scott@bighead studio.com or (401) 465–6829. Just don't tell him how cool his sideshow oddities are—we wouldn't want him to get a big head.

Polly want a two-headed skull and collection of macabre sideshow props?

FLIPPING THE BIRD

In spite of his work at Big Head Studio, Scott Bonelli is perhaps most well-known for a small run-in he had in December 2003 with Cranston's mayor, Stephen Laffey. Mayor Laffey wanted to have Christmas decorations on the front lawn of city hall. He decided that private groups would be allowed to set up a religious display on city property as long as it was not paid for with city funds. The mayor had said that he welcomed all valid religions to take part in the display—it just had to be tasteful. Bonelli wasn't keen on the mayor being the arbiter of what was valid and tasteful, so he plotted a drive-by flamingoing.

Amid the nativity scene and giant menorah on the lawn of city hall, Bonelli snuck in at night and planted fifteen pink flamingos. Still, he wanted to make sure it was legal, so he also posted a sign that said, "Wishing you a festive Flamingo Day. In the spirit of the Great Flamingo, spread love, peace, and frivolity to your neighbors, and to the world! A message from the Church of the Pink Flamingo. This Flamingo Day display has been brought to the citizens of Cranston at no cost to the city tax payers." Thus he aligned his flamingos with a religion, and assured everyone that the display was not paid for with city funds. It only remained for the mayor to decide if the flamingo display was valid or tasteful, and Laffey knew that barring the flamingos would probably cause more trouble than it was worth.

The ACLU still got involved and tried to stop the display, citing separation of church and state as the reason why religious displays shouldn't be shown off at city hall. But Laffey managed to win that battle, which no doubt would have been more difficult if he had allowed a nativity scene but banned the flamingos. The holiday display was able to remain on the city hall lawn, and came back the following year as well. As for the flamingos, they too have appeared on the city lawn each year, albeit in smaller numbers, and often sporting little Santa hats. What could be more tasteful than that?

Charity's Big Name

Cranston

When it comes to philanthropy and charitable giving in Rhode Island, there's one name that everyone knows, and that name is Alan Shawn Feinstein. Though he may not have quite as much cash as Warren Buffet or Bill Gates, Feinstein has donated a staggering amount of money to charity, giving millions and millions of dollars to scholarship funds, local schools and colleges, and various philanthropic organizations all over the country. Feinstein supports a wide range of educational and community service programs in Rhode Island, but his primary mission is fighting hunger. He is responsible for the Feinstein World Hunger Program at Brown University, the Feinstein International Famine Center at Tufts University, and the Feinstein Center for Hunger Free America at the University of Rhode Island.

One could argue that this incredible humanitarian generosity is the reason most Rhode Islanders know Alan Shawn Feinstein's name. But one could also argue that the reason everyone in Rhode Island knows Alan Shawn Feinstein's name is because he believes in putting it everywhere.

In 1991 Alan Shawn Feinstein founded the Feinstein Foundation in Cranston to help end hunger in America. In addition to the aforementioned programs, Feinstein has created the Feinstein Youth Hunger Brigade and the Feinstein Leadership Scholarships for students who have participated in any Feinstein Good Deeds or Feinstein Youth Hunger Brigade programs. He donated $5 million to found the Feinstein Institute for Public Service at Providence College, and donated $1 million to each of six Rhode Island colleges and universities for the Feinstein Enriching America Program. Doctoral students at the University of Rhode Island or Rhode Island College can do community service in his doctoral program to become Feinstein Fellows. In 1994 Feinstein founded the first high school based around community service: the Feinstein High School in Providence.

Okay, so many philanthropists put their name on things to which they donate—look at Andrew Carnegie. But Feinstein goes a bit further. His motto, "Helping to better the lives of others is the greatest of all achievements," is plastered on all public high school and middle school buildings in Providence, along with his name, Alan Shawn Feinstein. The Feinstein IMAX theater graces the Providence Place Mall, his name and face appear at bus stops, and billboards over the highway spell out ALAN SHAWN FEINSTEIN in big letters, along with a quote or picture. Alan Shawn Feinstein's name is ubiquitous, and he likes it that way.

Critics have charged that Feinstein is more interested in putting his name on signs than he is in helping people. Feinstein argues that anonymous donations don't inspire people to follow suit, and that by associating his name (Alan Shawn Feinstein) with his donations, he gives people something to emulate (Alan Shawn Feinstein). While peo-

For the amount of money he's donated, I'd let him put his name on my forehead.

"Helping to better the lives of others is the greatest of all achievements"
Alan Shawn Feinstein

ple may debate Feinstein's true motivations for keeping his name in lights, his commitment to philanthropy cannot be denied. He quit his job to become a philanthropist full-time in 1996, and by donating countless millions to Rhode Island schools and hunger-fighting organizations around the world, he has helped many people and earned the admiration of almost everyone—even those Rhode Islanders who feel that he should be less obsessed with his name, Alan Shawn Feinstein.

Beer Necessities
Cranston

The greatest brewery in all of New England is . . . well, actually, it's probably not in Rhode Island. But it used to be. In decades past there was no beer more popular than Narragansett Beer. It was possibly the most popular beer ever in New England. During the 1950s and '60s, Narragansett Beer accounted for nearly two-thirds of all beer sales in New England. No company has numbers like that today. But beer from the Narragansett Brewery had two things going for it.

First, there was the catchy slogan, "Hi, Neighbor, have a 'Gansett!" Okay, maybe wasn't that catchy, but it was catchier when it was announced by the Boston Red Sox announcer of the era, Curt Gowdy, which brings us to the other thing going for it. Narragansett Beer was a big sponsor of the Red Sox for two decades, and one of the first sponsors on television. Really, there are few things you can do that will endear you to New Englanders more than allying yourself with the Red Sox.

The Narragansett Brewery began in the late nineteenth century when a half-dozen local businessmen decided to open a brewery. Amazingly enough, they were all part German. (What are the odds?) Aside from the German brewmaster knowledge, the beer was pure Rhode Island, brewed and bottled in Cranston. In 1914 the plant modernized and became the largest lager brewery in New England. (There wasn't a larger lager.) Things went well until the company was sold in 1965, and production eventually moved to Indiana in 1981. Everyone agreed that the beer didn't taste nearly as good, and the once-unrivaled Narragansett Beer was no more.

That could have been how the story ended, but Narragansett Beer meant too much to Rhode Islanders. Mark Hellendrung of Providence, former president of Nantucket Nectars, decided to track down one of the brewmasters from the Narragansett Brewery to reclaim the old recipe. He has revitalized the brand, and although it's technically still not brewed in Rhode Island, at least it's owned by a Rhode Islander. And the brewery is not forgotten. Hazel Turley of Jamestown is brewing up a book about the Narragansett Brewery. She didn't ever work there, or even drink much beer, but while in her twenties and thirties, living in Rhode Island meant coexisting with Narragansett Beer.

Meanwhile, if you'd like to learn more about Narragansett Beer now, you can visit www.narragansettbeer.net.

Del-icious
Cranston

Some people say, when life gives you lemons, make lemonade. But Rhode Islanders know that when life gives you lemons, you should make Del's instead. What's Del's? Why, it's the quintessential summer drink in Rhode Island, a popular brand of frozen lemonade. Actually, popular doesn't quite do it justice. Del's is to frozen lemonade what Band-Aids are to adhesive bandages and Jell-O is to gelatin. Sure, there are other brands out there, but Del's is the one everyone knows, and any other frozen lemonade is likely to be called Del's as well. So what is

Nothing says summer like frozen lemonade.

frozen lemonade? Well, it's a cross between lemonade, a lemon sorbet, and a lemon slush, basically consisting of lemons, crushed ice, sugar, and two scoops of good-tasting magic.

Del's is practically synonymous with summer in Rhode Island. In addition to the stores, trucks and carts of Del's are everywhere, from the parks to the zoo to the sports fields. The state's favorite filmmakers, the Farrelly Brothers, have showed people drinking Del's in their movies, like *There's Something About Mary* and *Me, Myself & Irene,* to capture the feeling of summer in Rhode Island. After all, a summer in Rhode Island without Del's would be like a wedding with no cake. In fact, when it came time to vote for Rhode Island's state drink, Del's was a close second place, narrowly defeated by coffee milk. But if the vote had taken place on a hot summer's day, it's likely that the results would have been the other way around.

Del's can trace its history back through many generations, to a man named DeLucia in Naples, Italy. Starting in 1840, DeLucia would insulate the winter snows in nearby caves, then mix them with sugar and fresh lemon juice in the summer. His creation was sold at the local market, and it was very popular. His son, Franco DeLucia, came to America at the turn of the twentieth century and brought the recipe with him. Unfortunately, between rationing due to World War II and the work required to hand-crank the lemonade, selling it was a tricky proposition. Franco's son Angelo managed to create a machine that could automatically produce the frozen lemonade, so in 1948 the two of them opened a Del's Frozen Lemonade stand on Oaklawn Avenue in Cranston, next to the bowling alley they owned.

It was the beginning of a dynasty. Not only did the lemonade bring more people into the non-air-conditioned bowling alley during hot summers, but the lemonade itself was staggeringly popular. Angelo ended up selling the bowling alley in 1955, and decided that the stand should be supplemented by a pair of Del's Lemonade trucks that would, like ice-cream trucks, drive around town looking for overheated, thirsty people. In 1961 Angelo opened a second stationary location, and let one of his drivers run it. This was the first of many successful franchises. By the time Angelo's son, Bruce, entered the family business in the late 1960s, there were already five franchises in Rhode Island.

Today Bruce DeLucia is president of the company, and there are more than forty franchises, less than half of which are in Rhode Island. Del's has expanded through New England to sell products in some thirty-six states, and has even reached as far as Japan. Del's may have been served at the 1996 Summer Olympics in Atlanta, but the best place to get some is still Rhode Island, where carts and trucks are well-nigh ubiquitous during the warmer months. There's nothing better than a Del's frozen lemonade on a hot day. There are other flavors like watermelon and cherry, but the original lemon remains the best. If you want to make some yourself, you can order some mix online at www.dels.com.

All Greek to Me
Cranston

The annual Greek Festival at Cranston's Greek Orthodox Annunciation Church is a celebration of heritage. Rhode Island has many small groups with a unique heritage, but the Greek Festival may be my favorite. It's not due to their rich religious and spiritual heritage, or even the costumed dancing in celebration of their cultural heritage. No, my favorite thing about the Greek Festival is the heritage of tasty, tasty food.

Unlike some cultural festivals that order their food from outside vendors, everything at Annunciation Church's Greek Festival is made by volunteers from the parish. This includes the gyros, the souvlaki, and most importantly, the pastries. There are nine kinds of homemade pastries, many made fresh during the festival. Various delicious relatives of the baklava family are available, but the discerning palate will join me in favoring the galatoboureko, a wonderful custard pastry with no real equivalent.

For those of a less gastronomical bent, the traditional dancing is also quite entertaining, and also done by Annunciation Church parishioners. In fact, the whole festival is run entirely by volunteers, 150 of them in fifteen teams with chairmen working hard to bring everything together. They also bring *everyone* together, building a community within the parish.

The celebrating started nearly a century ago, but it was twenty-three years ago that the parish council decided to make it a festival open to the public. Father Andrew George, the priest of the church, remembers that everyone agreed that opening the festival was a good idea. "It helps present our heritage to the greater community," he says. "It's a lot of work, but a lot of fun."

If you'd like to join in the fun, the Greek Festival is traditionally held on the weekend closest to September 8, in celebration of the Virgin Mary's birth. It all happens at the Greek Orthodox Annunciation Church, 175 Oaklawn Avenue, Cranston.

Ready to Rock
Cumberland

Many states have a state rock. But Rhode Island's state rock, unlike slate or granite, is found only in Rhode Island in the town of Cumberland. It is named, imaginatively enough, Cumberlandite. It was originally named Rhodose because it could only be found in Rhode Island. But then people poking around the rest of the state realized it was even less common than they originally thought, so it was renamed as Cumberlandite. (I've never met-a-mor-phical naming committee.)

Cumberlandite itself is a porphyritic igneous rock classified as a variety of ferrogubbro composed of plagioclase feldspar crystals in a groundmass of mixed composition including magnetite. In English, that means that Cumberlandite was made by a volcano, contains many different minerals, and is somewhat magnetic. In fact, the mix of two dozen minerals in Cumberlandite has led it to be noticed over the years. The Nipmuck Indians reportedly viewed it as a sacred stone, and modern rock hounds often mistake it for a meteorite. And who can blame them? No other place on earth has the Cumberlandite, so you can understand their sediments.

Centuries ago, people tried to make cannons from Cumberlandite, but the iron content was insufficient, so it had to be smelted with iron ores from Cranston. Some people decried it as a worthless mineral. Now, of course, Cumberlandite has come into its own. Ever since the resolution declaring it the state rock of Rhode Island, nobody has taken Cumberlandite for granite. The source of Cumberlandite is known as Iron Mine Hill, and the nearly four acres it covers are thought by some to be the purest body of ore in New England. More than three and a half acres of a rare meteoresque ore composed of two dozen minerals, and all unique to Rhode Island? It's official: Cumberlandite rocks.

School Daze
Glocester

If there's one thing that children like even less than broccoli, it's school. Consequently, they enjoy any opportunity to get out of school, whether it be a vacation or pretending to be sick. But the best reason of all is the unexpected reprieve in the form of a snow day—a day when school is suddenly cancelled due to the weather. And there are two communities in Rhode Island that are famed for having far more snow days than anywhere else: Foster and Glocester. In fact, most people who don't live near them don't even know that the two are separate places, because they are used to always hearing them in the same breath.

Welcome to
GLOCESTER
GLOCESTER BUSINESS ASSOCIATION

Trust me, half of the state appends Fosta—in front of that sign.

People growing up in Rhode Island would listen to the radio any winter morning when there was more than an inch or two of snow, wondering whether their school district had decided to shut down the schools for that day. And as the announcer listed the closings, children eagerly listened in hopes of hearing their own school mentioned, which would essentially mean a free vacation day. (Parents also listened eagerly, hoping NOT to hear their school mentioned, because then they wouldn't know what to do with the kids when they went to work.) Some places like East Greenwich never closed, or at least it seemed that way when I was a kid growing up. Some places like Cranston West would close occasionally. But at the end of the list, one could count on hearing "Foster-Glocester" as having closed due to snow once again. Children across the state would enviously dream of attending a school that seemed to close during winter almost as much as it closed during summer.

When the weather gets snowy and cool,
Hearing radio voices is cruel.
We all miss Salty Brine
With his most famous line
When he'd say, "Foster-Glocester: No School!"

But while many local radio stations announced school closings, real Rhode Islanders knew that there was only one station to listen to in the mornings for closings, and that was 630 WPRO–AM. The reason to listen to this station was a character named Salty Brine, who hosted the morning show from 1943 to 1993. During this era Salty Brine not only hosted the WPRO morning show, but did commercials for local businesses and even hosted his own TV children's show, *Salty Brine's Shack,* for more than a dozen years. Yet in spite of all this, Salty Brine was most famous for three words: *No School FostahGlostah*. He would list each other school closing, and then always end on that one, with his traditional Rhode Island accent.

After he retired from the radio show, people would still ask him to say, "No School FostahGlostah," as it became as much a part of his personality as "Ayyyyyyyy" was for the Fonz. Sadly, Salty Brine died in 2004—but his immortal line lives on. And throughout Rhode Island, whenever anyone is listening to school closings, chances are that when they hear the inevitable "No school, Foster-Glocester," they think of him.

Gimme an A!
Johnston

There are few towns that love politics more than Johnston. And a large reason for that was their town administrator Mario aRussillo and long-serving mayor Ralph aRusso. Before he was mayor, the man's name was just Ralph Russo. So what's in a name? Well, in 1964 Russo and Russillo both wanted to run for office. Most people looking to impress tend to add letters to the end of their names, not the beginning. But Rhode Island law at the time said that after endorsed candidates, the rest of the field must appear on the ballot alphabetically.

Fearing that voters wouldn't bother reading through to the *Rs* for positions they didn't care about, both men worked together to change their names before the election. Russo and Russillo became aRusso and aRussillo, respectively. aRussillo won as Johnston's new town administrator, but aRusso sadly didn't win his bid for a state senate seat.

But the story gets much better. A few years later, aRusso and aRussillo were both competing for the town administrator position. And as if that weren't enough, the other candidates were named Acciardo, Anderson, and Arcand. Clearly, there was only one thing to do: aRussillo added a second *a* in front of his name, becoming Mario aaRussillo.

Apparently it was effective, because he managed to beat all the other A-people and win the election. However, aaRussillo didn't run again in 1970, and Ralph aRusso became town administrator.

aRusso held that position for eight years, and after the position of town administrator was upgraded to mayor, for another twenty-four years. Mayor aRusso was a man who didn't let go—not only of the position, but also of the *a*. In 1995 Russillo dropped the *a*'s from his name and became Mario Russillo once more. But Ralph aRusso proudly kept his *a* right up to his death in 1999. So while Russillo may be remembered without the extra letters, any longtime resident of Johnston will proudly tell you about Mayor aRusso. In Johnston history, as he tried to be on their ballots, aRusso remains first.

Art to A-maize

Johnston

Stephen Salisbury is a bit of an artist. Each year he creates a new work of art, and in 2006 his masterpiece paid homage to Vincent van Gogh's Starry Night. Certainly he is not the first artist to offer tribute to van Gogh, but there is something that makes his art special. His masterpieces are so large that you can lose yourself in them—literally. Salisbury's canvas is more than five acres of corn on his family farm, and when his annual creations are complete, they serve as gigantic mazes for visitors to run through from the inside trying to find the way out. (Why do the visitors run? Maybe someone's stalking them.)

For nearly a decade now, Salisbury has been designing and building an original corn maze every year. Though there are certainly other corn mazes around, the Salisbury Farm maze has two things that set it apart from the rest. First, it was the area's first corn maze. Many others have popped up since it began, but Stephen Salisbury first made a corn maze in early 1998, before everyone else. More importantly, he takes pride in designing the mazes with a new theme in mind each year.

When he originally decided to make a corn maze, various enterprising individuals attempted to sell him premade patterns and offered to cut the maze for him—for a price. After considering this for a bit, Stephen decided there was no reason he couldn't do it himself. Each year he thinks of an idea, whether it's an eagle or other patriotic sym-

Stephen Salisbury, a farmer who is outstanding in his field. Literally.

bols, or the witches of *Macbeth*, or great masterpieces of classical art. Then with the help of his brother Keith, who lives across the street from the farm, he designs the maze, and the two of them set to work building it. The maze also includes informative signs, so you can learn a bit about van Gogh while you're walking through a corny version of one of his paintings.

Of course, there's a lot more at Salisbury Farm than the maze. After all, the farm was founded by Salisburys back in the 1800s, and Stephen and Keith are the sixth generation of Salisburys to work on the farm, with their father, Wayne. In fact, their children already help out on the farm, so you could say that seven generations of Salisburys have worked the farm. The secret of their success? Not making it all about fun.

Seriously. Salisbury Farm has been a hay farm and a dairy farm, and today lets visitors pick their own pumpkins and strawberries. But one thing they won't offer is an overly festive atmosphere. Stephen insists, "We're a family farm, not a carnival." Which means that if you bring your kids, they'll appreciate the homemade candy apples, hayrides, and, of course, the corn maze, but the old post-and-beam barn will help them realize they're still at a farm, not just an amusement park with food. In other words, just because they've got a maize maze doesn't mean they want to be corny.

You'll find Salisbury Farm on Route 14 in Johnston. For more information call (401) 942-9741.

Need a Lift?

Johnston

Yankee Supply Company, at 2140 Hartford Avenue in Johnston, may not be the world's largest supplier of warehouse supplies. But they do supply the largest hand truck you've ever seen, which you can't miss if you drive past it on Route 6, because it's nearly a dozen feet tall.

Built more than a decade ago as an advertisement for Yankee Supply, this towering hand truck is theoretically functional and not just a model, though nobody on earth exists that is large enough to operate it effectively. Still, if a race of giants ever lands here and needs to start moving around compact cars, this is probably the first place they'll look.

Straight out of Paul Bunyan's garage.

Sedimental Journey
Lincoln

If you were driving down Route 116 through Lincoln, it's likely you'd pass a lot of rocks and a lot of lawns. But there's one lawn that has a lot of rocks arranged in a way that you shouldn't just take for granite. Most people driving by will do a double take. Some will even pull over to the side to take a closer look. And if you're lucky, you can catch the creator of these stone sculptures, Maria Alfieri.

Maria and her family of rocks.

Maria was born in Bolivia, where she used to make the stone sculptures with her mother when she was young. And before you ask, no, it isn't a Bolivian tradition. It is *her* tradition, playing with stones ever since she was a little girl. The stone sculptures represent a strong family—not only because the stones themselves are a family tradition, but because the large stones represent strength and the arrangement of little stones represents family. Each of her sculptures consist of one large stone as a base, with many smaller stones arranged carefully on top of it. Maria places the stones lovingly, with no glue or cement, so they occasionally fall off. But she picks up and fixes the stones every day, rearranging them like she did back in Bolivia. "I love stones," says Maria. "I love playing with stones. I can spend hours . . . "

The biggest sculpture in her collection, the first one she made, was based on a stone that she found completely buried in her yard. When the stone was unearthed, Maria arranged many stones on top of it. In addition to the various cars driving by, her sculpture attracted the attention of the crew doing construction on Route 116 near her house. She asked the boss at the construction site whether she could have a large stone to use as the base for a second sculpture. He said yes, and she placed more little stones on top to create another sculpture. When the boss saw this, he wanted to help her out more, and told her, "Just label the ones you want." And now her house number is written on various big stones that she plans to turn into more sculptures, including one across the street.

With her front yard already fairly full of stones, Maria shows no sign of diminished enthusiasm for acquiring more stones and building more stone sculptures. "My son and husband say, 'Enough with the stones,' but I love them. I want them in the house!" Thankfully for her family, the stones haven't taken over the inside of the house—yet. But the number of sculptures on her lawn continues to grow, with donated large stones from the construction boss.

Passersby will frequently wave or give her the thumbs-up if they notice her in the yard with her sculptures. After all, anyone driving by can see the truth as soon as they lay eyes upon Maria and her sculptures: They rock.

Mightier Than the Sword
Lincoln

If you've ever been writing with one of those cheap little white and blue ballpoint pens and it stopped working (they always stop working), you may have thrown the pen in frustration. And someone might have said, "Don't be cross." This is good advice if it was intended for you, but it's terrible advice for the pen. In fact, if only the pen had been Cross, the problem may never have happened.

Cross, after all, is Lincoln's famous pen factory. The A. T. Cross Company was created back in 1846 and is America's first manufacturer of upscale writing instruments. They also claim to be the last independent manufacturer of fine writing instruments in the country, and all of their pens are still made right in Rhode Island. The company has accumulated nearly two dozen patents for various pen and pencil technologies over the years, usually for prototypes of today's commonly used pens. For example, Cross developed the propel-repel pencil and the Stylographic pen, which although they have been outmoded by the mechanical pencil and the ballpoint pen, were quite clever in their time.

Richard Cross founded the company in Providence years ago, making upscale gold and silver casings for wooden pencils. He passed the company on to his son A. T., who then sold it to an employee named Boss in 1916 (and no, there was never a boss there named Employee). The Boss family remains the boss family to this day, having provided both the current and previous chairmen of the board. What's the result of having a company run by a former employee? A boss who lets any employee reject a product if it looks faulty. You know what they say: You can cross your boss, and you can boss your Cross, but don't cross the Boss who's the boss of Cross.

Milk in Your Coffee? Coffee in Your Milk!

Lincoln

If coffee isn't your cup of tea, or even your cup of coffee, you may be pleasantly surprised when you try coffee milk. Of course, if you're from Rhode Island, it's no surprise at all: You've probably been drinking the stuff for years. After all, it's part of our culture. Coffee milk is one of the standard options along with regular milk and chocolate milk. They have it in all the stores. They have it at the Dunkin' Donuts on every corner. They even have it in school cafeterias.

And yet, most out-of-staters are entirely unfamiliar with this delectable mix of milk and coffee syrup. But one supposes that's inevitable when Lincoln, Rhode Island, plays host to essentially the only company in the world that produces coffee syrup: Autocrat.

Autocrat coffee has been around since the 1890s, but it was only in 1940 that the company started making coffee syrup. And though for decades there was competition brewing in the coffee syrup business from a company called Eclipse, Autocrat acquired them in 1991 to become the sole coffee syrup supplier of the land. Eclipse had so many loyal drinkers that Autocrat still produces that company's recipe under the Eclipse name, but all coffee syrup nowadays is really made by Autocrat.

So what's the only thing better than being the sole supplier of the nectar of the gods? Having coffee milk named the state drink of Rhode Island, in 1993. It's that kind of thing that makes former Rhode Islanders the world over feel a patriotic duty to buy coffee syrup so they can raise a glass of Rhode Island's state drink to honor the motherland. If that desire takes over you, or even if you're just a benighted soul who wants to taste glory, you can order coffee syrup by giving Autocrat a buzz at 1–800–AUTOCRAT.

Rhode Island's state drink. A swallow will tell you.

Drive-In Miss Daisy
North Smithfield

Back in the 1950s, drive-in movie theaters were the place to be. Before VCRs and cable TV, if you wanted to see a movie with your family, or with a few friends, or especially with a hot date that you were excited about, the only place to go that made sense was the drive-in. Sadly, the glory days of the 1950s are gone, and nowadays many of the drive-in theaters have died out. But if you're in Rhode Island and you want to return to the majestic days of yesteryear, you have two choices: 1) Use a time machine and go back to the 1950s, or 2) Visit the Rustic Tri-View Drive-In in North Smithfield.

The only place in Rhode Island you can still drive-in to see a movie. Or three.

It's not quite as flashy as having a time machine, but it's cheaper and a lot more accessible. The Rustic Tri-View is now the last operating drive-in movie theater in Rhode Island. The state has a grand tradition of drive-in theaters—one of the first ten drive-ins anywhere in the world opened in Providence in 1937 (named, surprisingly enough, the Providence Drive-In). After the end of World War II, people were in the mood for entertainment, so drive-ins proliferated during the 1950s. The Rustic Drive-In itself opened in 1951 (with only a single screen at the time), and by the 1960s there were well over a dozen drive-in theaters operating just in Rhode Island and more than 4,000 around the country.

But the 1970s and '80s were less kind to drive-in theaters, and between cable TV, VCRs, improved indoor theaters, and booming real estate prices, many drive-ins died out. Only one in Rhode Island was able to weather the storm, and that was the Rustic Drive-In. The Rustic received a grand revitalization in 1988 when it was purchased by Clem and Beverly Desmaris. Why were they so eager to own a business that seemed to be part of a fading era? Simple: The two of them had first met at that same drive-in thirty-four years earlier, in 1954. Unwilling to let the Rustic Drive-In disappear, they decided to make it better than ever. They added AM and FM radio broadcasting of the movie audio, as well as two more screens. Thus, the Rustic Drive-In became the Rustic Tri-View Drive-In.

These days the Rustic can accommodate 550 cars, and still tends to fill up on Saturday nights with good weather. And why wouldn't it? People have a certain nostalgia for the drive-in theaters of their youth, and there's a whole different atmosphere than in a traditional theater. Kids can run around and throw Frisbees before the movie. You can smoke in your car as much as you like, or talk through the entire movie. And, of course, entry is priced by the car, not the person. If you're looking to take your family or friends out to a movie, $17 a car is a lot cheaper than you'll pay at the traditional theaters—especially because you can cram as many people into the car as you can fit.

It's advantages like this that explain why people are willing to drive an hour or more just to visit the Rustic during its season from April through September. With three screens, two of which almost always feature first-run movies, you have a good set of choices. In fact, if you get there early to grab one of the best spots, you can park between two screens so your kids can watch one movie and you can watch another. And with the movies playing and Frisbees flying while you sit outside and eat some clam fritters, you may forget that you didn't opt to use the time machine.

The Rustic Tri-View Drive-In is located on Route 146 (Eddie Dowling Highway) in North Smithfield. Call (401) 769–7601 for more information.

Spoiled Milk

North Smithfield

Sometimes you come across an old building and say, "I wonder what that used to be used for?" Some buildings are very mysterious. Others are slightly more obvious, such as the gigantic milk jug building on Route 146 in North Smithfield.

To the surprise of very few people, the building used to be an ice-cream stand. What is surprising is that this is not the original location of the building. After the old ice-cream shop shut down, the building was moved here and was supposed to reopen. Unfortunately, there were some issues (rumor has it, issues of the septic variety), and the grand renaissance never arrived.

Still, as you drive down the highway, you may as well appreciate the building, even if it is all boarded up. After all, there's no use crying over spilt milk.

We're sorry this building closed. Dairy, dairy sorry.

Carving Out a Niche
Pawtucket

Carving a pumpkin is relatively simple. You take a big knife and cut two holes for the eyes, a hole for the nose, and a mouth. But if you were carving pumpkins for the Jack-O-Lantern Spectacular, there would be two reasons your carvings would take longer. First of all, your carvings would have to be much more elaborate. And second, the team you were part of would need to carve roughly 5,000 pumpkins. Because the annual Jack-O-Lantern Spectacular absolutely requires thousands of pumpkins; otherwise, they'd call it the Jack-O-Lantern Mediocre.

The Spectacular has been going on for almost two decades now, having been created by John Reckner in 1988. Back then there were fewer than 200 pumpkins, mostly just carved by people who lived near Reckner in Oxford, Massachusetts, where the one-night event was first held in the back of a school. A few hundred people showed up, and the event was a success. People's appreciation drove Reckner to make the event bigger and better, which drove more people to appreciate it (and they drove their friends to go see it, too). Ultimately, near the end of the twentieth century, the Spectacular had grown to a weeklong event with 4,000 pumpkins. Reckner faced an overwhelming task of carving, indeed!

Enter Providence's Roger Williams Park Zoo, which offered to host the Spectacular in the new millennium. Reckner managed to get a team of professional pumpkin carvers to assist him, and things were more spectacular than ever. Attendance nearly quadrupled, and Reckner refined his strategy. A few weeks before the event opens, carvers are divided into teams. Some scoop out pumpkins, others outline the complex carvings, and some just do "filler." What's filler, you ask? Filler means all the "normal" jack-o-lanterns, like the kind you carve at home with your family. The experts turn them out in a few minutes each, which is what you have to do when you're making a few thousand of them to take up space. The real time is spent on the complex carvings, which range from detailed facial portraits of presidents like Woodrow Wilson to pop stars like Michael Jackson.

After hosting the Spectacular for a few years, the zoo decided to pass in 2006, so it was moved to McCoy Stadium in Pawtucket. If possible, it became even more spectacular, not only adding a plethora of baseball stars, but also audio accompaniment beyond the standard music for many of the themed displays. Nothing can quite describe listening to "Who's on First?" while viewing perfect likenesses of Abbott and Costello's heads carved into pumpkins, all while standing on a baseball field. Behind home plate was a tremendous pumpkin tree bearing a menagerie of menacing jack-o-lanterns, made all the more evil by the spooky laughter-laced theme music playing.

At the time of this writing, it's not clear where the 150,000-plus pounds of jack-o-lanterns will end up in 2007. But it is clear that you should go see them.

Extra Innings
Pawtucket

Quick, how many innings in a baseball game?

If you answered nine, you probably weren't at McCoy Stadium on April 19, 1981, because that was the location and date of baseball's longest game—ever. Actually, that's not quite technically accurate. The date wasn't just April 19, it was also April 20. And also June 23. By the time the game finally ended, it had gone on for eight and a half hours and thirty-three innings.

It all began normally enough. The Pawtucket Red Sox were hosting the Rochester Red Wings for a minor-league AAA game at McCoy Stadium. There was a slight delay due to some lighting problems, but the game started at 8:00 P.M. It went scoreless for six innings, with the Red Wings scoring a run at the top of the seventh inning. There were no more runs scored until the bottom of the ninth, when the Paw Sox managed a run to tie the game.

And that's where the trouble started.

The game continued, scoreless, for inning after inning after inning. Nine scoreless innings went by, the length of an entire second baseball game. Still, the score remained tied at 1–1, and the players continued to tire.

Another two scoreless innings went by, and then in the top of the twenty-first, Rochester scored a second run. Finally, it looked like the game would end. But Wade Boggs, who would go on to be a big star for the Boston Red Sox, hit an RBI in the bottom of the twenty-first to tie the game once more.

At first the Paw Sox were excited to have tied the score, but then they began to groan when they realized that they had just missed their chance to go home. Never has a baseball team been less excited to score a run. After all, it was already one o'clock in the morning. But now the score was tied 2–2, and the game continued.

Note that the game should not have continued—the International League rules state that no inning in a minor-league AAA game is supposed to start past 12:50 A.M. But due to a cruel twist of fate, the umpire's copy of the rulebook was missing this rule. The umpire tried to call the president of the International League, but couldn't get through. Meanwhile, the game continued.

And once again, another nine scoreless innings went by. By now the players had been playing continuously through the equivalent of more than three games. Two more scoreless innings went by. And then the league president finally picked up his phone. He was astonished to learn that the game was still going on, and demanded it be postponed at the end of the inning.

Finally, at 4:07 in the morning at the end of the thirty-second inning, play finally stopped. Only nineteen fans had stayed up all night to watch the game, and they were rewarded for their stamina with free season tickets from Pawtucket—because, clearly, they hadn't watched enough baseball. But the score was still tied at 2–2, so the game remained unfinished.

Two months later, on June 23, Rochester's team returned to Pawtucket to finish the game. Thousands of people showed up to see this historic event, which was even heavily covered by the national sports news—rare for a minor-league game.

The best baseball stadium in the world, home of the longest baseball game in the world.

And then, in the blink of an eye, it was over. In stark contrast to the eight-hour, two-day marathon of the April portion of the game, it took only one inning and eighteen minutes to end it in June. At the bottom of the thirty-third inning, Paw Sox player Dave Koza was called to the plate with the bases loaded, and drove home the winning run.

Thus was baseball's longest game finally over—but not forgotten. Many of the players from that night went on to the major league, like Wade Boggs and Cal Ripken Jr., but they all remember it vividly. History remembers it because it set a host of records. Not only was it the longest baseball game ever, but it also had the most at bats, most strikeouts, most pitches thrown, and so on and so forth. And McCoy Stadium commemorates this historic event by having the box score not only painted on the wall, but also around the rim of the cups they serve soda in. So when you're watching a Paw Sox game, you can have fun by turning your cup around and looking at the endless progression of ones and zeros.

Truth be told, it's probably more fun than if you'd been there to see the real thing.

> April 19th was this game's beginning,
> But 'twas June by the 33rd inning.
> And what could be more fun
> Than to have played and run
> In the world's longest baseball game? Winning!

THE REAL MCCOY

McCoy Stadium is the home of the Pawtucket Red Sox—the best stadium and the best baseball team anywhere in the entire world. Granted, my view may be slightly biased by the fact that when I was growing up, my summers were always filled with trips to McCoy Stadium to see baseball games. And I even got to go out on the field once! Nonetheless, objective facts will speak to McCoy Stadium's greatness.

It began with Pawtucket mayor Thomas McCoy, who supported the plan to build a stadium when it was first suggested back in 1938. (Clever readers will be able to deduce where the stadium got its name.) McCoy laid the cornerstone of the foundation in 1940, on a site called Hammond's Pond. Most people would shirk away from building a baseball stadium on top of a swamp, but those fears were baseless. The stadium was completed in 1942, and in 1946 it was finally named after the man who had championed it—Mr. Stadium. No, it was, of course, named for Mayor McCoy, and McCoy Stadium began hosting minor-league baseball that same year.

McCoy hosted a small farm team, was empty for a few years, hosted another farm team, and was empty once more. But in 1970 the Boston Red Sox brought their AA minor-league team to McCoy, where they have stayed ever since. Three years after arriving, the team was promoted to the AAA International League, and now boasts the oldest stadium in that league.

Of course, old stadiums need repairing, so a vast renovation of McCoy Stadium took place in the 1990s. Almost everything was improved, from the sod and the seats to the lighting and the

CONTINUED

restrooms. Most importantly, the seating capacity was almost doubled, from 5,800 to more than 10,000. And that has let even more fans come to the best stadium in the world. Why else is McCoy the best stadium in the world? Because it creates exciting baseball. Whether it's an outfielder trying to catch a ball in the league's largest foul territory, or a baseball flying over the 8-foot outfield fence for a home run, the games are exciting.

Better yet, the Paw Sox has been the starting point for many of the Boston Red Sox's most famous players, from old Hall of Famers like Wade Boggs to more recent players like Roger Clemens and Mo Vaughn. And you can see the players up close and personal, since the seats are all very close to the action, even up in the bleachers. The dugouts are literally dug out underneath the stands, but that doesn't stop the fans from getting autographs. At every Paw Sox game, you'll see kids (and a few adults) lined up along the front of the stands, holding strings attached to hollowed-out milk jugs, soda bottles, or whatever they can find. The baseball cards or other assorted things for signing are put into the bottles, the fans lower the ropes, and the players sign the things and then let the fans pull them back up.

And here's the best part: General admission is only $6.00 for adults and $4.00 for kids. Where else can you see major-league-caliber baseball for $20 for a family of four? Of course, if you're feeling rich, you can spring for the box seats at $9.00 a pop. But wherever you sit, you'll have a great view. After all, you're at the best stadium in the world.

You Say You Want a Revolution
Pawtucket

What's that? You thought the American Industrial Revolution started in some big state with tons of factories? Now wait just a cotton-pickin' minute—and then wait for a few more cotton-refinin' minutes. Because there's one man who can be credited with starting the Industrial Revolution in America, and that man is Samuel Slater. Slater went to Pawtucket in 1793 where he built the first mechanized factory and textile mill in the country, and called it, surprisingly enough, Slater Mill.

Slater Mill was the first mass-production textile mill in America, harnessing waterpower with its giant wheel to produce cotton yarn. Slater didn't stop with his first mill either; once he had a few dozen employees, he began building around the mill. Putting up housing allowed him to attract families, especially those who needed money. This was

Slater Mill: Home of the Industrial Revolution.

handy, as many of his employees were children, since their smaller hands tended to be useful for small adjustments where adult hands might be too big. See? Handy.

He went on to buy land farther down the river and build another mill there, in a place that he called Slatersville. (Samuel Slater: a great innovator in mass production, not an innovator in naming towns.) There he not only built housing, but a company store, schools, and even churches. Once all of his workers lived in the town he created, he could pay them with company credit (usable at the company store) rather than cash. So, along with the Industrial Revolution, Slater brought the first company town to America. Anyway, back at the site of the first Slater Mill, another mill was eventually built in 1810, named the Wilkinson Mill. This was a somewhat larger mill that boasted stone walls less flammable than the Slater Mill and a machine shop on the bottom floor that made parts for the mill (and Slater Mill, and other mills) to run. Both the Wilkinson Mill and the Slater Mill remain at the same site to this day, and have working machinery that you can see. Technically, the Wilkinson Mill's eight-ton waterwheel is a reproduction, but if you watch all the pulleys and leather belts whir and process cotton, you'd never know it wasn't the original machinery.

And you can actually go right into the mills and see the machines in action, as part of Slater Mill's twenty-first-century improvements. Slater Mill is open to the public seven days a week, from May through September. And they have staff who dress in period costumes and make touring the mill much more interactive, sharing the occasional yarn about life in the nineteenth century. They'll demonstrate the finest in eighteenth- and nineteenth-century technology, and occasionally let you turn a crank as well, if you're nice.

In addition to the Wilkinson and Slater Mills, the Slater Mill site includes the Sylvanus Brown House. The Brown House offers a look at home life during the olden days, to weave in some context to the mill life. To take a guided tour of all three of these old buildings only costs a few dollars. But you can save a dollar by printing out a coupon from their Web site at www.slatermill.org.

The Slater Mill site is at 67 Roosevelt Avenue in Pawtucket. For more information visit the Web site or call (401) 725–8638.

Hot Potato
Pawtucket

Idaho may be the state most famous for potatoes, but Rhode Island is the state that thought of sticking eyes in the potatoes. Okay, potatoes already have eyes. But we added ears, a nose, a mouth, and voilà—Mr. Potato Head, a collection of facial features to make your spud into more than just a common tater. This beloved children's toy was invented by George Lerner in the late 1940s and sold to Rhode Islanders Henry and Merril Hassenfeld of Hassenfeld Brothers, later shortened to Hasbro. They released Mr. Potato Head to the public in 1952, and it became an overnight success—earning more than $4 million for Hasbro within its first year alone. Part of this may have been due to the fact that it was the first toy ever to be sold through national television advertising, but the genius of the idea cannot be denied.

Originally, it was just a box of face parts designed to be stuck into a potato, but as the Irish know, you can't always depend on having a potato around. So, in 1964, Hasbro began packaging a plastic potato with the kit. In 1974 the plastic potato was horribly changed, not only doubling in size, but also no longer allowing would-be Picassos to put noses in the eye sockets. In 1987 they finally realized the error of their ways, and began producing plastic potatoes that were a friend of creativity once more. The range of accessories has dwindled over the years, with the most notable disappearance being the pipe, after much

Soviet Russia, Potato cooks you!

lobbying from the American Cancer Society.

In spite of this, Mr. Potato Head remained smokin' hot. His fame has continued to grow over the years, appearing in a comic strip by Garfield cartoonist Jim Davis, a television show on Fox, commercials for Burger King, and both *Toy Story* movies. But nothing compares to the thrill of seeing a life-size Mr. Potato Head in person. In 2000 Mr. Potato Head was named the official Family Travel Ambassador of the state. And to show off just what a friendly ambassador he is, thirty-seven customized life-size Mr. Potato Heads were created and installed around the state. Potato Heads represented included everyone from the

> *The Picasso potato creator:*
> *When it comes to toy spuds, there's none greater.*
> *'Tis a marvelous thing*
> *And unlike Larry King,*
> *It's decidedly no common tater.*

Independent Spud (a golden homage to the Independent Man atop the State House) to Edgar Allen Poe-tato. In 2002 Mr. Potato Head celebrated his fiftieth birthday by appearing on specially ordered Rhode Island license plates. But as a serious-minded individual, Mr. Potato Head also took advantage of his fiftieth birthday to receive an AARP card, and that's no joke.

Sadly, many of the life-size potatoes have since moved on, so you may never see figures like Spud Light or the Surfer Spud, but some of them are still around. And nothing's better than a 6-foot potato holding food. If you want to see Mr. Potato Head for yourself, you'll find him outside Hasbro's main office at 1027 Newport Avenue, Pawtucket.

DON'T TOY WITH ME

Rhode Island is the funnest place in the world. That's right, funnest. It may not be a real word, but it means big fun for kids. Because kids love toys, and nobody produces more toys than Rhode Island's famous toy company, Hasbro (unless you count Mattel, which we don't.

Hasbro makes classic toys like Mr. Potato Head, various games, and most importantly, really cool toys that blow things up with a variety of guns, like GI Joe and Transformers. You might say they have a monopoly in the toy biz—actually, they publish Monopoly, too.

Old Folk Home
Pawtucket

One of Rhode Island's best venues for music is called Stone Soup. But in spite of the name, it's not rock music. No, Stone Soup is a coffeehouse that has hosted folk musicians for more than a quarter century, and it's one of the most well-known folk music venues in New England. How well-known? Well-known enough that everyone from Richard Shindell to Patty Larkin to Rosalie Sorrels to Mr. Folk Music himself, Pete Seeger, has played there. Yes, on pretty much any non-summer Saturday, you can drop by the Stone Soup Coffeehouse and hear yourself some great folk music.

Of course, just because the folk music will be great doesn't mean that it will be by someone famous. In addition to the bigger names, Stone Soup hosts a number of talented but less famous folk musicians who may be traveling through the area. And most importantly, Stone Soup also presents a vast array of local folk musicians like Atwater-Donnelly and Pendragon. Why? Because the main purpose of Stone Soup is to promote folk music, a purpose that it fulfills by boosting the cornucopia of talented folk musicians in the Rhode Island area.

You might think that focusing on helping local artists instead of just presenting big names would make Stone Soup less profitable than it could be. You'd be right. Stone Soup is, in fact, a nonprofit organization. It was founded by Richard Walton, whose name you may remember because he ran for vice president in 2004 on the Ralph Nader ticket. Actually, you probably wouldn't remember his name for that. But you should remember his name for creating this wonderful nonprofit group with a real social conscience. Each season begins with a Labor and Ethnic Festival, and the Stone Soup Coffeehouse continues to attract people with its mission of keeping the folk arts community alive.

And it's a good thing they attract people, because not only is Stone Soup nonprofit, but it is entirely run by volunteers.

Best yet, you can be one of those volunteers! In addition to chatting with other like-minded folk-appreciating volunteers like yourself, you get free admission to the show, and sometimes get to chat with the performers as well. All you have to do is move a few chairs around, help in the kitchen, and work the merchandise table. You can do as few or as many shows as you like—just be sure to show up if you've signed up. Spots tend to fill up fast, especially for the bigger names, so you'll want to sign up in advance by calling the volunteer coordinator at (401) 461–7687 or e-mailing volunteer@soup.org.

If you're not volunteering, ticket prices are still very reasonable. Performances happen Saturday nights at 8:00 P.M. from Labor Day to Memorial Day, with a few exceptions. The schedule is online at www.soup.org, which will even tell you which nights have an open mic before the main attraction. And one more thing—although the proud tradition of Stone Soup had been at the Slater Mill for many years, they moved to St. Paul's Episcopal Church, 50 Park Place, in February 2006. So when you show up, be sure it's the right place, or you'll just sit around stewing.

Here Be Dragons
Pawtucket

You may dismiss water dragons as myth, but every year in Pawtucket, you can see them with your own eyes. Granted, these dragons are technically boats, but they are still resplendent with a furious visage as they make their way across the water for the annual Taiwan Day Festival. Historically, these races took place to ensure a good harvest and drive away evil spirits; nowadays, they are simply modeled after the famous Dragon Boat Festivals elsewhere in the world. But don't think they aren't authentic—over the years the Taiwanese government has donated nearly $100,000 worth of equipment to the city of Pawtucket for their Taiwan Day celebrations, including some genuine

If you were a demon, these boats would scare you.

Taiwanese–style dragon boats (one of the few times you're excited to know something was made in Taiwan).

The boats each take a steersperson, twenty paddlers, and a drummer to keep the tempo. Watching the painted dragons race literally neck and neck towards the finish line is fairly entertaining. But better yet, you don't have to just sit as a spectator. If you can gather a group of twenty people who are over eighteen and know how to swim, you can borrow a boat and join the races. Sure, there's a small entry fee of $600 per boat, but in addition to lending you a dragon boat and all the necessary equipment, everyone on your team gets a T-shirt and pizza. And you get to tell people you rode a dragon.

Whether you feel like taking up an oar or just eating Chinese food while you watch the dragons battle, the Taiwan Day Festival has been making September exciting in Pawtucket since the turn of the millennium. If you want more information about this year's festival, contact the Blackstone Valley Tourism Council at 1–800–841–0910.

Clip and Save and Save
Woonsocket

If you've ever gone shopping and managed to get something for only half of what it normally costs, you know the great joy that comes from buying things at a discount. And if you managed to get something for only a quarter as much as it normally costs, then you'd probably be thrilled. But you'd also still be a complete amateur compared to Carol Ochaba, because she is the Coupon Queen.

What qualifies her to be the Coupon Queen? Well, she routinely uses coupons to buy ridiculously large amounts of groceries for ridiculously small amounts of money. Sure, you probably think your mom is good at using coupons, because she saves them all the time and once got four of something for the price of one. I used to think that, too. But Carol Ochaba takes using coupons to a whole other level. She walks into a store and buys $166.00 worth of groceries for $1.75. That's not a typo. That's less than $2.00 for well over $150.00 worth of groceries. And another time she bought $581.00 worth of groceries for only $19.50. Most people would boggle at the idea of getting nearly $600.00 worth of groceries for under twenty bucks. What did Ochaba have to say about it? "If it wasn't for the tax, they would have owed me money instead."

Being the Coupon Queen is similar to being a superhero. Ochaba has been on television as her super-identity, but also takes a normal job during the day to throw super-villains off the trail. She has worked as a waitress at Chan's restaurant in Woonsocket since 1963. She plans to finish out an even fifty years before quitting, because she still loves the job, and has been there longer than anyone else. But once she does quit, she can still take in money with her yard sales. Ochaba buys many $3.00 items at 25 cents apiece, and sells them for a dollar each in big sales.

What's Carol Ochaba's favorite thing to buy? Whatever's on the biggest sale.

How does one prepare to be Coupon Queen? The most important thing, unsurprisingly, is to have lots and lots and lots of coupons. Ochaba has shoeboxes filled with coupons at home, and even has a handful with her when randomly accosted during a day at work. She has a contact at the newspaper and gets sixty to seventy copies of the good coupon sections, and then staples all the same coupons together. She waits until something like toothpaste is on sale for a dollar a tube and she has a dollar-off coupon, then she buys sixty tubes of it for only the cost of tax.

The Coupon Queen brings shopping to a whole new level. It takes patience to save that much money, but anyone who has been working at the same restaurant for nearly fifty years clearly has the patience. And she plans to continue using her coupon-powers to obtain extremely discounted bags full of merchandise. I think the best way to sum up Carol Ochaba's mindset is with an offhand comment she made while discussing her coupons: "I hate to buy things for more than 25 cents."

Egg Rolls and Drum Rolls
Woonsocket

Fish and bicycles. Peanut butter and pickles. Toasters and frogs. If these all seem like natural pairings to you, then you won't be at all surprised that one of Rhode Island's most well-known restaurants is famous for its combination of Chinese food and jazz. Chan's Fine Oriental Dining, at 267 Main Street in Woonsocket, serves up moo shu pork with a side order of blues (which is odd, because China is more famous for being red). Though the restaurant has been around since 1905, the Chan family didn't take ownership until 1965. And while they have won awards for having the best Chinese food in Rhode Island, the real excitement at Chan's is the jazz.

Since the 1970s jazz artists from all over the world have played at Chan's, from Roomful of Blues to the great Dizzy Gillespie. Once the music started becoming as much of a draw as the food, Chan decided to expand the restaurant into a full-fledged jazz club. Although you might not be able to tell from the outside, the restaurant has now doubled in size from what it once was. The classic Chinese decor is accented with photographs and posters from famous people who have dined there, from *Saturday Night Live*'s G. E. Smith to the Farrelly Brothers, famous writer/directors of such hits as *There's Something About Mary* and *Dumb and Dumber*.

And the music hasn't stopped. Live jazz is available at Chan's every weekend, and many people have begun to come to Chan's Fine Oriental Cuisine without any intent of sampling the cuisine. This is a shame, as

For those who prefer their Chinese food with something other than Muzak.

their menu has everything from pupu platters to these shrimp in a delicious black bean sauce . . . but I digress. Those who are not interested in the culinary menu will be glad to know that the entertainment menu has been expanded as well. In addition to jazz, the club now features blues, folk, cabaret, and even comedy performances. The only downside? An hour after you hear the jazz, you'll be hungry for more.

They're open daily, but if you're planning to go on a jazz night, you'd best make a reservation by calling (401) 765–1900.

Side by Each
Woonsocket

Rhode Island has a dialect, to be sure. There are accents, there are dropped r's, and there are words like bubblah that few other states use. But even within Rhode Island, there is a region that has a dialect all its own, and that region is Woonsocket. Woonsocket, in fact, is probably best known for the bizarre speech patterns that prevailed there during the twentieth century. Phrases like "side by each" instead of "side by side," or "Throw me down the stairs my coat" instead of "Throw my coat down the stairs to me." This is because the population of Woonsocket is largely French or French-Canadian. How French? Well, let's just say that some people call it la ville la plus française aux États-Unis, which in case you didn't notice, is French. Oh, also, it means "the French-est city in the United States."

So how did it get so French? Well, after the Industrial Revolution, many textile mills popped up in the area. Communities of immigrants formed around the mill, villages formed out of those communities, and Woonsocket was formed out of those villages. Now, of course, not all of those immigrants were French. The majority of them were French or French-Canadian, but many were not. However, the number of French-speaking immigrants was so overwhelming that most of the non-French immigrant workers who moved there ended up learning French. They learned English as well, but the influence of the French on the language was clear to hear.

And that's why Woonsocket is known for people saying things like "Drive slow your car" or "I'm taking a walk, me." The unique Woonsocket dialect has been remarked upon by many authors, perhaps most notably Mark Patinkin and Don Bosquet in their *Rhode Island Dictionary*. This humorous book about Rhode Island culture took a section to make fun of the Woonsocket dialect, which aroused the ire of a few people in the region, who wrote to the state paper to complain. However, the complaints were soon outgunned by the many letters from Woonsocket residents who had a sense of humor about their speech.

Sadly, as the generations go by, this speech pattern is starting to disappear. While it used to be that everyone in the region talked like this, these days only the older residents of the city say things like "I live on top of my sister." Even though more than 46 percent of the population identified themselves as French or French-Canadian in a census at the end of the twentieth century, the younger generation is now more likely to talk with the common slang of today's American youth than with the Woonsocket dialect of their grandparents. But many of the grandparents are still there, so if you visit Woonsocket, you're still likely to be able to hear the famous Woonsocket phraseology for another few years.

After all, it is *la ville la plus française aux États-Unis (peut-être sauf Louisiana)*.

BRISTOL COUNTY

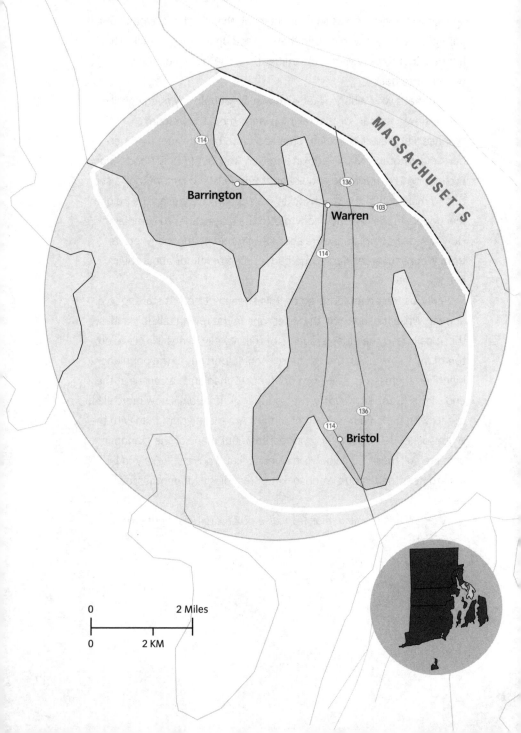

MASSACHUSETTS

114

Barrington

136

Warren

103

114

114

136

Bristol

0   2 Miles

0   2 KM

BRISTOL COUNTY

A Real Cool Moose
Barrington

You've probably heard of Teddy Roosevelt's Bull Moose Party, but you may not be familiar with Rhode Island's Cool Moose Party. Third-party candidates always have trouble finding support in a country where the two-party system is so entrenched, and Barrington resident Bob Healey is no exception. He first founded the Cool Moose Party and ran for governor in 1986. Although his bid was unsuccessful, he ran again in 1994 and received almost 10 percent of the vote, forcing the state to recognize the Cool Moose Party as an actual political party.

Bob Healey is famous for his slogans. His winning run for Warren School Committee chairman used the slogan "A Strange Man for a Strange Job." And his unsuccessful gubernatorial bid had the slogan "Healey for Governor . . . Why not? You've done worse." But his true genius lies in his slogans for the lieutenant governor position, like "The best lieutenant governor you'll never have." Why *never* have? Because Healey's platform for lieutenant governor consists of a single issue: eliminating the position entirely.

The only official legal responsibility of the lieutenant governor is to take over for the governor if necessary. And for this, the position costs the state three-quarters of a million dollars every year. Healey argues that this is a ridiculous waste of money, and is running for the position in order to eliminate it. This may seem like a joke, especially when backed by slogans like "Nothing for me, thanks," "No work, no pay," and my personal favorite, "Bob Healey for Lt. Governor: He won't be there for you." But Healey is quite serious about running for the position to eliminate it. In his 2002 bid for lieutenant governor, he managed to win 20 percent of the votes, even against an incumbent.

He announced his 2006 bid for lieutenant governor from Uruguay, and explained that this action only proves his main point—namely, that "no matter where you are in the world, and no matter what you are doing, you can also be serving as Rhode Island's Lieutenant Governor at the same time." Having failed to win the election in previous years on a more serious platform, Healey decided to build a platform

If Bob Healy should win for the post,
The position would soon become toast.
He'll do nothing, you see,
But he'll do it for free;
Most officials could not make that boast.

with a bit more absurdity in 2006. But behind all the bluster, he really is serious about wasting less of other people's money. "I have no plans for the office of Lt. Governor, and, in fact, will not maintain a staff nor take a pay for my service. I don't want the money and I really don't need a job. Rhode Island doesn't need this job but really does need the money," says Healey.

He not only desires no staff and no pay for the position if he wins, but in 2006 asked those wishing to contribute to his campaign to donate to charity instead, because he does not need the money. Healey does say that he is willing and able to govern if he wins and is subsequently called upon to do so, but sees no reason to take $750,000 from Rhode Island's coffers just to wait for someone to die. As he's said, "Under the current Rhode Island Constitution, the only role for the lieutenant governor is to wait for the death or incapacity of the governor.

Since this is the only constitutionally assigned job, I propose to do it four times faster . . . I will be four times more diligent about waiting for the governor's demise."

And we'll be diligently watching Bob Healey, to see what happens next. You can follow him at www.votehealey.com.

Mystery Museum
Bristol

The Musee Patamecanique in Bristol is a wonderful place. And I'd love to tell you exactly where it is, but I can't. Seriously. The museum's creator, curator, and tour guide, Neil Salley, does not like to reveal the location of his museum. Suffice to say it is in Bristol, and if you decide to make an appointment for a tour, only then will the museum's location be divulged.

Salley invented the word *patemechanics* during his time at the Rhode Island School of Design, and his museum is a collection of what he calls *patemechanical* objects. He describes these as artifacts displayed to validate the existence of other realms and allow us to envision them—basically, objects that go beyond the bounds of the reality of this world.

So what kinds of objects would these be? Wonder-cabinets of insects, a time machine, and items to intrigue all of the senses. Sights, sounds, even smells are produced by the patamechanical machines while Salley serves as eager tour guide. You can see a swirling neosma of letters and lights, or even grab hold and give a few turns to the Crank-O-Wank. Drawings and complicated descriptions of the exhibits are available online at Salley's Web site, www.museepata.org. These drawings do not do justice to the experience of being guided through the actual exhibits under operation, but you'll have to visit the Web site anyway if you want to visit the museum itself. Tours are by appointment only, and appointments are by e-mail only.

Tours are available from 6:30 to 9:00 P.M., Tuesday through Friday, and limited to eight people. But look on the bright side: You can be sure there will be no crowds. Nobody else even knows where it is.

Flower Power
Bristol

The groundskeepers at Blithewold Mansion, Garden & Arboretum really like daffodils. Or at least when it comes to April, they had better learn to like daffodils, because April is the time of year for Blithewold's annual Daffodil Days celebration, where 50,000 daffodils are in bloom all over the grounds. And if those weren't enough flowers for you, there are also various perennials like forsythia around the grounds, in addition to century-old greenhouses showing off cuttings, seedlings, and citrus plants. But really, if 50,000 daffodils aren't enough for you, you probably need help.

Well, if anyone can help you with greenery, it's the gardeners at Blithewold. The place is all about the plants and trees; the word *blithewold* even means "happy woodland" in Old English. The name was given to the estate by owners Augustus and Bessie Van Wickle. Bessie hired a New York Parks superintendent named John DeWolf to turn Blithewold into a horticultural wonder. The two of them added everything from a vegetable garden to a giant sequoia, and when Bessie died, her daughter Marjorie moved into Blithewold to continue developing the arboretum.

Marjorie died in 1976, leaving her estate to be enjoyed by the public. In 1999 a group called Save Blithewold Inc. took over maintenance of the mansion and gardens. Currently there are three full-time garden

staff responsible for the greenery of Blithewold. So how do they manage all of it themselves? Simple: They don't. The three gardeners are
assisted by two dozen volunteers who maintain the gardens, divided
into groups of Rockettes, Florabundas, and Deadheads (no, they aren't
Jerry Garcia fans; they just remove dead flowers from the plants on the
grounds).

How many daffodils are in this picture? Start counting, we'll wait . . .

Anyway, the gardens are open to the public year-round—rock garden, water garden, and all. The mansion (actually the second mansion; the first one burned down in 1906) is open from April 16 to Columbus Day, Wednesday through Sunday. Each room of the mansion contains a detailed history, as well as various floral arrangements. But if you really like flowers, you should go between April 16 and 30, because those are Daffodil Days. Not only can you see 50,000 daffodils out in the gardens, but if you go on a Wednesday, Thursday, or Friday afternoon during Daffodil Days, you can even have a proper afternoon tea in the Blithewold dining room.

Blithewold is located at 101 Ferry Road (Route 114) in Bristol. For more information call (401) 253–2707 or visit www.blithewold.org.

Putting His Heart into It
Bristol

Steve Brosnihan has been a professional cartoonist for more than twenty years, and like most cartoonists, he puts his heart into his work. But unlike most cartoonists, he also wants you to put your heart into it as well. More specifically, Brosnihan is a tremendous believer in organ donation. This is why, for the past thirteen years, everything he's drawn includes a little message in four words: "Be an organ donor." These words appear beneath his cartoons in the paper, on the sweatshirts he sells, and even beneath his own logo on his business card.

How did Brosnihan get so interested in organ donation? Simple: He started hanging around the people who need them. He has been the resident cartoonist at the Providence Hasbro Children's Hospital for fifteen years, and hence has gotten to spend a lot of time with kids whose lives depend on organ transplants. After well over a decade drawing for, and with, these children, he's become one of the state's most outspoken supporters of organ donation. But just like a winning basketball coach, Brosnihan urges you to give 110 percent, because in addition to writing "Be an organ donor" on all of his published cartoons, he has also done work supporting blood donation. And tissue donation. And marrow donation. And various other causes we're not even going to list because there are too many of them.

But Steve Brosnihan isn't popular in Rhode Island because he's a charitable man. He's popular because he draws fun cartoons. This is a great advancement for him, because before becoming a cartoonist, drawing cartoons got him in trouble. As a student at Dartmouth College, he was supposed to be focusing on design instead of cartoons, which is why he would be reprimanded for turning in work that was plagued by cartoons. Thankfully, he now works for the *Providence Phoenix,* a newspaper that is always happy to see Brosnihan's cartoons.

His most famous cartoons are probably his rebuses. Brosnihan has created and drawn rebuses to represent every town in Rhode Island, and has assembled them into something he calls "Rhode Island . . . can be puzzling." I remember many years ago at a town fair where I first saw shirts on display with these rebuses, and I puzzled over them . . . a scholarly-looking man holding a book saying "college," plus the letter *E,* plus a dinged-up car with arrows pointing to the dings? What could that be? Teacher E Bashed Up Car? Professor E Smashcar? Professor E Dents? Prof. E Dents? Providence!

Naturally, I ended up buying the shirt. I won't spoil any of the other rebuses for you, because while the cartoons are pretty, half the fun is in working them out yourself. So if you want to get yourself some rebuses, just head over to Steve's Web site at www.stevebcartoons.com; write P.O. Box 111, Bristol, RI 02809; or call (401) 253–5909. His company is called Fly by Knight Designs, so naturally the logo shows a medieval armored warrior alongside an insect of the species *Drosphilia*—a fly by knight. Hey, we told you the man liked rebuses.

MEASURING UP

In America, we generally use the English system of measurement. You weigh yourself in pounds, buy half-gallons of milk, and get your car checked out after so many miles. There's this other system out there called the "metric system" that foreign countries use, but America has never really liked the idea. The metric system is based on tens, so it's actually easier to use, but we find our system easy because it's familiar. The metric system also has the advantage of having prefixes that can quickly tell you how big something is, whereas our system has different words altogether. Inch, foot, yard, furlong, mile . . . but sometimes we run out of words, and no standard English measurement like mile is big enough.

That's where Rhode Island shines. For decades, newscasters and reporters around the country have been using the RhodeIsland as a unit of measurement. When talking about a small foreign country, the anchor will explain that it's twice the size of Rhode Island. Martian craters being explored are reported to be forty-three times the size of Rhode Island. Comparing things to Rhode Island is simply the best way for our country to understand large amounts of area. All that remains is for our government to admit that since we're not converting to metric, we need to adopt the RhodeIsland as an official unit of measurement.

In spite of the fact that this has yet to occur, Rhode Island continues to be used as the benchmark for large things across the globe. Meteorites, forest fires, newly discovered moon craters—all of them are dutifully reported in terms of their size in relation to Rhode Island. An iceberg 1,500 square miles large is not something the world can understand. An iceberg the size of Rhode Island is. Even other states (such as Texas) are often described in terms of how many times the size of Rhode Island they are.

Some states may take pride in being many times as large as Rhode Island, but it should be obvious to any impartial observer that the state most revered is the one everyone else feels the need to compare themselves to.

BRISTOL COUNTY

Patriot Act

Bristol

Quick, can you guess which state holds the longest-running Fourth of July celebration in the United States? If you guessed anything but Rhode Island, you really need to pay more attention to the theme of the book you're reading. Yes, the country's oldest Fourth of July celebration has been going on every year since 1785, and it takes place in a town called Bristol. The first celebration was directed by a Revolutionary War veteran named Reverend Doctor Henry Wight. Under Wight's direction, prayer was offered, speeches were given in praise of liberty and freedom, and music and military parades took to the streets as part of the exercise.

All things considered, it hasn't changed too much since then. They added a chief marshal for the parade in 1826, but aside from that, the same sort of celebration took place every year—or almost every year. There was no parade in 1881 because President Garfield had just been shot two days earlier, on July 2. As a sign of respect for the president, there was no parade that year. Other than that, the annual celebrations have continued right up to the present day, complete with prayer, speeches about freedom, and, of course, the parade.

Needless to say, some things do change over time, so a few of the less-important traditions have been replaced. The greasy pole climb disappeared about half a century ago, perhaps because watching a bunch of teenagers trying to mount a 30-foot-tall pole conjures up the wrong kind of associations for a family-friendly Fourth of July celebration. And the open fires were too unsafe to remain a part of the celebration, from the fires in barrels that used to burn all over town, to the giant communal bonfire that was discontinued just a few decades ago. But there are still lots of fireworks, so we haven't lost out on the opportunity to see things burning and exploding, and that's what's important.

What's more, there are a number of contests now associated with the parade, from photos and buttons to an essay contest for kids, a Miss Fourth of July title for young women and little girls, and even a presentation of a special prize to the Bristol-born person who has traveled the farthest to reach the celebration. What do they win? A U.S. flag that has flown over the U.S. Capitol. That's just one of the many, many flags around during the Bristol Fourth of July celebration. Sure, there are lots of flags at most July 4 celebrations,

Bristol during the Fourth of July: even more American than apple pie.

but there are even more here. Tiny flags everyone waves, larger flags flying from poles and banners, historic flags passed down from generation to generation, flags made of wool, flags from ships, flags on people's shirts, and so on and so forth. And the red, white, and blue doesn't stop with the flags; those colors are all over town—flowers, giant banners, people's clothes, paint on their faces, dye in their beards, a woman who dresses up in a Patriot missile costume . . . everything in Bristol is patriotic on the Fourth.

And, of course, there's the parade. The parade includes everything from traditional floats and marching bands to antique cars and a team of horses. Politicians, soldiers, children of veterans, beauty queens, clowns, and various mascots all march down that same road, every year. The parade is so popular that real estate in Bristol tends to cost more if it's on the parade route. It used to be that people who paid for these houses were rewarded by having random folks set up shop on their lawn at the end of June and stake it out days in advance, but in the early 1990s the town ruled that nobody can make any sort of claim on a parade-watching space before 5:00 A.M. on the day of the event. But you'd better believe that Bristol is a very tense town at 4:59 A.M., so if you plan to get a good spot to watch the country's oldest Fourth of July celebration and parade, don't be late.

For more information on Bristol's big day, visit www.july4thbristol ri.com.

Big Man, Little Boat
Warren

George Greenhalgh of Warren is energized by boats. In fact, boats make him so excited that he can lift a whole yacht with his own two hands. Well, okay, technically it's a model yacht, so it's slightly smaller and lighter than your standard full-size yacht. While an actual East Coast yacht will measure roughly 12 meters and take twelve men to operate, the EC-12 model yacht measures less than 2 meters in length and, conveniently, only takes one man to operate. And Greenhalgh has built and raced a few of them, as a longtime member of the Narragansett Model Yachting Association (NMYA).

Like many NMYA members, Greenhalgh used to be a sailor. He would live on the water and sail real boats: full-size yachts, a town-class sloop 17-footer, and all sorts of other craft. But as time went on, sailing became harder, and finding a willing crew wasn't always easy. Then fate intervened one day many years ago at a boat show. He was looking to buy a full-size J24 racing boat, but his eye fell upon the model boats—the EC-12, to be exact. Greenhalgh decided that the model boats would be just as fun, but require a lot less money and a lot less work.

He's now been building and racing model yachts for twenty-five years. There are roughly twenty members in the NMYA, buying hulls from registered dealers and then building the rest of the boats by themselves. The final boat must be approved under association guidelines before racing. The NMYA, which is a chapter of the American Model Yachting Association, almost disappeared a few years ago when some of the members died, but it's still sailing along today. In fact, almost every Sunday in Roger Williams Park in Providence, you can see Greenhalgh and three or four other NYMA members racing their model yachts around Elm Pond.

The scorekeeper is Greenhalgh's wife, Norma. Norma says model yachting just isn't her cup of tea, but she dutifully keeps score at all of George's Sunday matches. On his signal, she starts a tape with classical music, and an official voice calls out the time until mark in fifteen-second intervals, interspersed with an ominous ticking sound. During this time the boats jockey for position near the starting buoy, moving at speeds of up to 7 miles per hour. The action is, admittedly, also smaller than real life.

It's not the size of your boat that counts, it's how you use it.

But the models sail with all the same rules as the big boats, and Greenhalgh says that when you sail the model yachts, it feels like you're sailing a big one. He often relaxes in a chair near the edge of the pond while sailing, and isn't too competitive during the Sunday runs, but still concentrates very hard during the races and can't take his fingers off the controls. So don't try to talk to him during a race, because he'll have to ignore you. But he isn't being snobbish, he's just trying to delicately guide his boat around the course.

"Between the races," says Greenhalgh, "we're very nice people."

He has built nearly thirty boats over the years, and his favorite is whichever one he's currently working on. While continuing to build his own boats in his garage, he has also helped many other hobbyists. And while there are few things that George Greenhalgh loves more than building and racing boats, one of them is hearing from other model yacht enthusiasts that he might have helped in the past, and keeping the hobby alive for others. So if you remember George from the time he gave you great advice for your sails, or especially if you want to join the Narragansett Model Yachting Association, don't hesitate to give him a call at (401) 245–7493.

Aqua-Man

Warren

Whenever there's something going on in Rhode Island that has to do with the state's waters, Luther Blount of Warren probably knows about it. In fact, there's a 50–50 shot that he has something to do with it. Luther is the owner of Blount Boats, and is a man who has always loved the water. Not only the water, but the things that live in it, and the things that ride on top of it. Blount grew up working for his uncle, who was in the oyster biz. In high school he built rigs for canoes, built a kayak for duck-hunting, and converted rowboats to sailboats. This interest in boats led him to engineering and mechanical arts courses in college.

After college he ended up on dry land, at a textile mill. But his mind was still on the water. In 1941 oysters and quahogs were fished from the sea and hand-opened with knives, even by the big firms. Blount had an idea to change that, and suggested that the 50-square-foot pressure cookers his mill used for cotton might be adapted to steam open the quahogs. The quahog man was unconvinced, arguing that the shells would probably shatter, and nobody wants shattered shell shard seafood. But Blount wouldn't let the idea go. He suggested a second tank of water in which a huge chain-mesh bag would hold the quahogs, and then briefly be dropped into the first tank to receive fifteen pounds of steam pressure—enough to open but not shatter the quahogs. He drew up the plans and sold the patent, revolutionizing the mollusk industry.

Blount also worked on boats with his brother. He eventually created Blount Marine in 1949, and began building and selling boats. One of the secrets to his success is that Blount always comes up with new ideas. He holds more than twenty patents on fishing and boat improvements, ranging from the very first flushless toilet to various pieces of the stern trawler. If imitation is a form of flattery, then Luther Blount has been very, very flattered—everyone else in the boatbuilding business tended to copy his ideas, because he kept building things better. And building better boats is what Blount continued to do. He's built 320 vessels over the years, with two more under way.

While delivering some of his boats on the Erie Canal, Blount decided that passenger boats would be fun. He was the first to start cruises on small boats (65 feet or so) rather than big ships, back in 1969. He built a second one in 1971, and ran boats from Chicago all the way down the Mississippi that were short enough to go under the bridges and could carry people while they slept. His small cruise ships were ahead of their time, and since he was the only game in town for a while, it earned him a lot of money.

The man behind many boats, in front of many boats.

BRISTOL COUNTY

And what does a man who loves Rhode Island's waters do with all that money? Why, he funds things to make people appreciate the waters, naturally. In 1976 Blount bought some land around Prudence Island with a creek that ran from the island past the road. One day he noticed that one side of the road was higher than the other during high tide, and the road created nearly seventy-eight acres of marsh. This gave Blount an idea. He built a pond in the marsh and a pipe to bring lots of water across the road—four million gallons each tide. The movement of the tide provided oxygen that allowed oysters to thrive, and numerous oysters on a string were placed into these waters to repopulate them. While clams were once in danger of disappearing from local waters, Blount's work has helped ensure that this won't happen.

"I wanted to do something that would last," says Blount. And to show he meant it, he donated $700,000 to endow a fund to manage this conservation effort even after he has passed on. More than twenty-five years after this fund was created, the oyster population is healthy, and the fund continues to keep it that way. Blount is also a very generous donor to a few local colleges with marine science programs. Ninety-year-old Luther Blount still shows up to work at the same office and desk that he's been at for more than fifty years, since 1954. Surrounded by pictures of some of the many boats he has built, he knows then when it comes to Rhode Island's waters, he has truly made a splash.

NOTE: After this piece was written, Luther Blount died in September 2006 at the age of ninety. But he is remembered as the man who put the town of Warren on the map, the man who made boats and cruise lines to help people visit the rest of the map, and the man who helped local waters so they meant more than just blue on a map.

Plumpkin
Warren

Quick, what's orange, weighs half a ton, and can either be deliciously sweet or have a scary face? A giant pumpkin. And if you want to see giant pumpkins, there's no better place than the annual Rhode Island Southern New England Giant Pumpkin Growers Championship, held each October at Frerichs Farm, at 43 Kinnicutt Avenue in Warren. The pumpkins there often weigh literally half a ton, and are lovingly tended by farmers throughout the year just so they can show them off.

Creating a giant pumpkin isn't easy. Farmers hoping to grow a competition-worthy one often spend hours each day tending to the pumpkins—cutting and burying vines, injecting the pumpkins with milk, sprinkling manure and other fertilizer on them, and watering them throughout the day. At night, many farmers take pains to protect the pumpkins from damage, whether with fences, dogs, or a vigilance that comes only from insomnia. And even after all that, there's no guarantee that the pumpkins will grow.

If your typical squash leaves you bored,
Come see Warren's gargantuan gourds.
People come every year,
Bringing huge pumpkins here,
And the biggest will win an award.

Just ask Scott Palmer of Coventry, who won the twelfth annual championship in 2005 with a 1,443-pound pumpkin. He set a New England record, and was only four pounds shy of breaking the world record at the time. But in 2006, despite months of careful monitoring and care, one of his pumpkins split and another went rotten, so Palmer ended up unable to enter the competition.

Even if you can't enter, the event is still entertaining. In addition to seeing some of the most gargantuan pumpkins in the world, you can be driven around in a pumpkin coach or find your way through mazes made of hay bales and corn. And, of course, there are refreshments. Just don't try eating any of the pumpkins that are still in the competition, or people will think you're out of your gourd.

For more information about this year's event, call Frerichs Farm at (401) 245–8245.

Small state. Big pumpkins.

DUEL PURPOSE

These days, if two people have a dispute, they usually hire lawyers and settle it in court. Centuries ago, people would sometimes have duels instead, which was a lot less messy. Duels started to fade in popularity in the 1800s, when most states had laws against them. Basically, the laws stated that a duel still counted as murder if you killed the other person, with the result that even if you won, you lost. (See how lawyers make things messier?)

But while most other states in the area had anti-duel laws on the books, Rhode Island had no such regulations (just one more way that Rogue's Island earned its name). Interestingly, of the five duels ever recorded in the state of Rhode Island, not a single one of them involved an actual resident of the state. Rather, parties in contention from other states would travel to Rhode Island to settle their differences, where they could do so without being arrested.

Ironically, as it turned out, none of them would have been arrested for murder anyway, because nobody was killed in any of the duels. The first duel ever recorded in the state of Rhode Island took place in March 1806. James Henderson Eliot believed that William Austin had written an article insulting his father. Both men traveled from Massachusetts to shoot it out, and Austin walked away wounded. The next recorded duel took place more than two decades later, in July 1827. The participants were two Frenchmen about whom little else is known, save that only one of them was wounded.

Perhaps the most entertaining duel took place in December 1832, when two men arrived from Massachusetts and eagerly inquired to make sure they had reached Rhode Island and not Connecticut, for fear of running afoul of that state's anti-dueling laws. But they needn't have worried, because the only injury either of them caused was when one of the men shot himself in the leg. A short time later, in January 1834, two men from Boston decided to fight over a woman in time-honored tradition. Bob Hooper met Shocko Jones on the battlefield, and Shocko Jones was wounded (and perhaps surprised).

The last recorded duel in Rhode Island took place in October 1835 between two New Yorkers—a state much more well-known for angry people. And they had more reason to be angry after the duel, as neither man killed his opponent, but both of them walked away wounded. Eventually, Rhode Island would also ban dueling, and people would no more travel from out of state to attempt to kill each other.

But remember, a Rhode Islander was never involved in any of these duels. We prefer to come at you from behind.

NEWPORT COUNTY

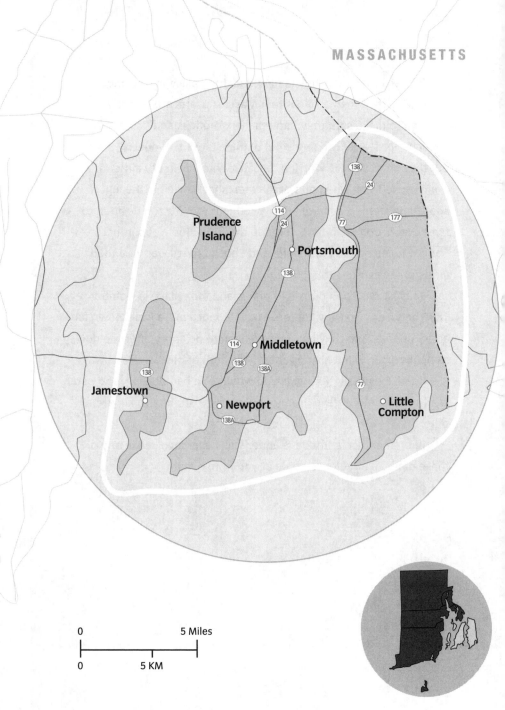

MASSACHUSETTS

Prudence
Island

Portsmouth

Middletown

Jamestown

Newport

Little
Compton

0   5 Miles

0   5 KM

NEWPORT COUNTY

Blowing in the Wind

Jamestown

Conanicut Island is the only part of Jamestown anyone ever seems to remember. Sure, there's also Dutch Island and Gould Island and a few other patches of rocks here and there, but if someone says something about Jamestown, there's a good chance they're talking about Conanicut Island. And if there's one landmark that best represents that island, it's the Jamestown Windmill.

The original windmill was built in 1728, and was used to grind corn by harnessing the winds coming off the ocean. They didn't really have many other options; modern power sources hadn't yet been invented, and there was no source of free-running water that could be harnessed to turn a waterwheel (the standard corn-grinding option at the time). The local Quaker fellowship moved their meetinghouse to Windmill Hill in 1734, because in addition to oats, apparently Quakers like corn, too. But while the windmill was first visited by Friends, it was soon beset by enemies, during the Revolutionary War.

On December 10, 1775, roughly 200 British and Hessian troops landed at East Ferry on Conanicut Island. (See, even the British only remember Conanicut Island.) They marched across the island to West Ferry, where they burned down the ferry house to start their swath of burning down buildings all the way back, including well over a dozen houses. Many residents fled to the mainland. A year later, another British fleet landed at

Narragansett Bay and took Newport, as well as taking over and occupying most of Jamestown until 1779, Conanicut Battery included. The British left in October 1779, once again burning down everything they could on their way out, from lighthouse to windmill.

Thankfully Jamestown recovered, and by the 1780s the Quaker meetinghouse, Beavertail lighthouse, and various other buildings were rebuilt—including the windmill, in 1787. It was immediately put back to work grinding corn, and continued to do so for well over a hundred years, until 1896. Though it's no longer grinding corn, the windmill still works to this day, and sits proudly in the center of Conanicut Island on Windmill Hill. The windmill is three stories tall, and made of chestnut beams and covered with shingles. Minor restoration was done in 1981, and major renovations in 2000–2001.

If you're a windmill fan and want to see this piece of history, just blow on in any weekend during the summer from 1:00 to 4:00 P.M. If you don't like those times, you can call (401) 423–1798 to set up an appointment for a different time with the Jamestown Historical Society. Either way, admission is free, so just pop on down to North Road and look for the big windmill. You really can't miss it.

It's just like being in Holland, only not.

Ship of Fools
Jamestown

Only a fool would attempt to build a ship out of half a car, a sofa, and a lot of underwear. And only a complete fool would attempt to sail such a boat in a race. No wonder, then, that the Jamestown Yacht Club's annual silly sailing event is called the Fools' Rules Regatta. The competition is entirely free and open to anyone of any age. The rules are simple: build a ship, on the beach, constructed entirely out of things that aren't manufactured for marine use. No inflatable dinghies, no surfboards, no actual sails. Boats must be constructed from random items people might have in their homes, like beer cans, a bathtub, and a sail stitched together from burlap sacks. The vessels must be propelled entirely by nature's wind, with no other means of propulsion, including paddling. Oh, and whoever builds the boat has to serve as the crew.

Building your own boat is just ducky.

Sound simple? Sure it does. And also hilarious. People will try to launch anything from plank-bearing water coolers to lawn chairs tied to balloons. The course is only 500 yards long, but many of the craft still don't make it the full way. After all, they have to be assembled on the beach, and they're made from complete random junk. Luckily, winning the race is not the only way to get an award. There are also three special awards: the Most Ingenious Design award, given to the best-designed craft; the Worst Example of Naval Architecture award, given to the worst-designed craft (which probably didn't make it all 500 yards); and the Judges' Award, given to the boat and crew with the best overall theme. Theme? Yeah, it usually involves costumes.

The nonsense all starts at the Town Beach at East Ferry, Jamestown, where a cannon is fired to signal the participants that they may begin constructing their watercraft. Two hours later, the races begin. The event only occurs once a year, but it's definitely worth seeing. You'd be a fool to miss it. For more information visit the Jamestown Yacht Club Web site at www.jyc.org or call (401) 423–1492.

Artistic Coffee
Little Compton

Sophisticated people tend to like things like drinking coffee and looking at art. So you might think the Art Cafe in Little Compton was created to appeal mainly to sophisticated people. And you'd be wrong. Sure, there's a coffeehouse, and a gallery, and even a garden and a patio, which would be enough to lure your average sophisticate. But Josie Richmond, owner of the gallery, definitely wanted to make it inviting to the world at large.

"I think art should be accessible to everyone," says Richmond. There are a few reasons you might be inclined to believe her. First of all, the gallery features works by nearly two dozen local artists, most of which is more likely to cost hundreds rather than thousands of dollars. Second, she used to be an art teacher, so making art accessible to people was her job. And perhaps most tellingly, there is a big chalkboard outside where children are encouraged to create their own art, as well as a few chalkboard tables made to be drawn on. That's art for the everyman, everywoman, and even everykid.

It's a cafe. It's an art gallery. It's a breath mint. Okay, it's not a breath mint.

If that still doesn't convince you that the art is for everyone, Richmond donates 10 percent of art sales to the Sakonnet Preservation Association, a local land trust. So at the very least, the art is for everyone local. A word of advice, though: If you show up at the gallery tomorrow morning, don't address the woman who works there as "Josie." Josie Richmond is often not present, so the gallery is looked after by her friend Judith Worthen, who owns the coffeehouse half of the Art Cafe. And don't try to pay with a credit card; they don't take them. Chalk it up to local charm.

The Art Cafe: A Gallery is located at 7 South of Commons Road in Little Compton. For hours and other information, call (401) 635–2169.

An Uncommon Commons
Little Compton

Across the street from the actual Commons in Little Compton sits a restaurant called the Commons Lunch. Since 1966 it has been serving up traditional Rhode Island fare, from stuffies (chopped quahog in the shell baked with peppers and breadcrumbs) to johnnycakes—and not the fat little silver-dollar johnnycakes either, but the large, extremely flat ones, made from white flint corn and delicate and lacy at the edges. I'm getting hungry just writing about it. In addition to the Rhode Island fare, Commons Lunch also serves up all kinds of other delicious food, from seafood like fried clams and lobster rolls to Italian food like veal and spaghetti and meatballs.

And who's responsible for all of this? None other than owner George Crowther, who has been running the restaurant since he opened it forty years ago. It has been very popular with both locals and vacationers, who come for not only the food but also the camaraderie. Commons

Lunch was a bastion of familiar comfort up until March 2004, when the restaurant burned down.

Crowther had talked about taking a vacation from the restaurant business for many years, and the burning down of the restaurant may have seemed like fate. But a few weeks later, he already felt that something was missing in his life. "It's like it's in your blood," said Crowther. "You just miss it, you know?" Other people missed it, too; he could hardly go anywhere without folks asking him when Commons Lunch would reopen. He soon decided that it was an important part of his life (and perhaps realized it was an important part of other people's lives as well), and embarked upon a quest to reopen. He ordered a new building from Canada, but was careful to keep the look very much the same.

The Commons Lunch is such an institution, even fire couldn't kill it.

After various delays due to struggling with permits, water, and contractors, Crowther finally reopened Commons Lunch on May 8, 2006. His wife, Barbara, was back making the desserts, from pastries to pies to puddings. (She may make something that doesn't begin with *p*, but you'd have to go there yourself to find out.) His daughter and son-in-law were assisting as well, and despite not advertising the grand reopening (unless you count the small sign hung on the door scrawled in black magic marker that mentioned the fact), more than four dozen people were lined up outside for the event. Crowther had served nearly 400 people by the time the day ended, and though he had tried to start small by just opening for lunch and dinner, by the following week he was already serving breakfast again as well.

Commons Lunch is back and better than ever, where "better" means "now serving beer and wine," which was not the case previously. The other draws, from the delectable johnnycakes to the homemade desserts, have not disappeared. The whole Crowther family is now involved with making Commons Lunch *the* place to go eat in Little Compton, so naturally, you should go eat there.

Commons Lunch (401–635–4388) is located at 48 Commons and is open from 6:00 A.M. to 7:00 P.M. every day, and an hour later on weekends. Just be sure to bring cash, as they don't accept credit cards.

What the Devil
Middletown

Sometimes it's fun to follow in the footsteps of great men. You can tour a house where Thomas Jefferson lived, or stick your hands in concrete where a famous actor once did the same. But if you go hiking in Purgatory Chasm, you can do one better—you'll be following the footsteps of the Devil himself. Legend has it that Purgatory Chasm is the spot where

Hobomoko killed a murderer. And no, Hobomoko isn't a new Japanese robot vagrant. It's the name for the Native American devil.

Anyway, long ago, Hobomoko supposedly found an Indian woman who had killed a white man. This occurred not at Purgatory Chasm, but at a location in North Kingston. The legend goes on to say that Hobomoko grabs the woman, stamps his feet once or twice, and then whisks her off to Purgatory Chasm, where he smashes her head into a rock, attacks her with an ax, and finally carries her over to the ledge and throws her into the waters.

This may sound unlikely, but proof remains right in the rock. There are round depressions in the rock where Hobomoko smashed the woman's head, sharp cuts in the rock where his weapon struck, and even a few devil's footprints in the stone on the path where he carried her to the edge. Of course, if you are more geologically minded, you might chalk all of these marks up to the ravages of time and to various cuts and marks that Mother Nature (a different kind of devil) just happened to put there.

Regardless of which devil did it, Purgatory Chasm is a large fissure that was formed by hundreds of years of wave action from the sea, causing erosion as well as some other interesting geological features. There's a conglomeration of various rock formations that have come together, beds of rocks that have been flattened and stretched out by millions of years of compression, and pockets of quartz separating different types of rock, giving further evidence of the squashing of rocks that went on ages ago. And all of this makes it a pretty neat place to go hike around—even if you don't run into the devil.

Purgatory Chasm is located on Purgatory Road in Middletown. Call (401) 847–7565 for more information.

DRIVING YOU CRAZY

People always complain about drivers in their state, from Florida to California. In Rhode Island, however, we have a right to complain, because we are officially the worst drivers in America. It's true. In 2005 GMAC Insurance took a nationwide survey to test drivers' knowledge of basic car safety and road rules. Out of fifty states, Rhode Island placed fiftieth. That's dead last, for those of you paying attention. The average score for a Rhode Islander taking the test was 77 percent, only a few points above failure.

A fluke, you say? Just bad luck in the first year of the survey? Well, a similar national survey was taken in 2006, and Rhode Island once again managed to place fiftieth. The average score dropped to just over 75 percent, and more than one-fourth of the Rhode Islanders surveyed failed the test entirely. This comes as little surprise to the author of this book, who during his driver's license exam, drove through a stop sign, made a left turn into the oncoming traffic lane, and nearly hit a parked car. I was surprised I passed, but I now understand that I am part of a proud tradition of Rhode Island drivers. Well, maybe just part of a tradition.

You're Soaking in It

Newport

The annual Save the Bay Swim from Newport to Jamestown in Narragansett Bay is probably the most logically-named fund-raiser there is. Sure, it's nice when people walk to cure cancer or buy baked goods to support a good cause, but once a year Save the Bay hosts a swim where people raise money for Narragansett Bay by actually swimming across it. Save the Bay, as you might have guessed, is an organization dedicated to preserving and restoring the environmental quality of Narragansett Bay. So why does the bay need saving?

Swimming across the Bay: A great idea for people in better shape than I am.

Glad you asked. Other people might have asked the same question, but they got their answer in 1977, at the very first Save the Bay Swim. A few days before the swim, the state Department of Health contacted the staff at Save the Bay to tell them that the water off Jamestown Beach was so polluted that nobody could safely swim there. The downside was that swimmers the first year had to row a few hundred feet offshore before getting into the water. The upside was that by doing so, everyone had a very good idea of why they were in the water in the first place. They were swimming now so they could swim without a boat later.

There have now been thirty Save the Bay Swims, with well over 400 people attending the 2006 event. The swimmers swim 1.7 miles from Newport to Jamestown, and include participants from fifteen-year-olds to seventy-nine-year-olds and everyone in between. Fast swimmers can finish the swim in a little over half an hour. Slower swimmers may take up to two hours. But it's not a race, it's a fund-raiser. And they must be putting the *fun* in fund-raiser, because some people just keep coming back to do the swim every year. Harold Schein, a seventy-one-year-old man from Narragansett, has done the swim twenty-nine of the thirty times it occurred. And it must be working, because Narragansett Bay is in much better shape than it was thirty years ago.

The whole thing started with Trudy Coxe, who was the assistant director of Save the Bay back in 1977. Having swum the bay herself in her youth, she decided to enlist nearly one hundred people to swim across it in a public event to raise awareness and money. So if you're fearless, determined, and athletic, maybe you want to swim in the next Save the Bay. Even people who need wheelchairs have done it. But if your idea of fun doesn't involve swimming 2 miles, you can watch other people do so instead, and maybe sponsor one of them. It'll help Narragansett Bay just as much, and it's a heck of a lot easier.

You can find more about Save the Bay, and their annual swim, at www.savebay.org.

Yacht's All, Folks

Newport

When your car needs restoring, you can ask for more information at a garage. But where do you go when your yacht needs restoring? Why, the International Yacht Restoration School (IYRS) in Newport, of course. Their graduates restore yachts all over the world, having taken courses in boatbuilding, marine systems, and, of course, classic boat restoration. This is all part of the IYRS philosophy that maritime knowledge and craftsmanship to build and restore classic boats should not be lost.

But talk is cheap. That's why the IYRS is also working on restoring the country's oldest yacht. The *Coronet* was built in 1885, and the plans are to restore it in a manner as faithful as possible to the original, using IYRS graduates as the main workers. Once complete, the *Coronet* is slated to be used as a floating museum of maritime history. Until it's ready to float around the coast, however, if you want to see the country's oldest yacht and the most qualified people to restore it, you'd better sail over to Newport.

The school is constantly receiving busted up classic yachts and restoring them not only for sail, but for sale as well. You can pay them a visit at 449 Thames Street, or call (401) 848–5777.

Meals on Wheels
Newport

I will not eat green eggs and ham. I would not, could not, on a train. But that's mainly because you can get much better food on the Newport Dinner Train. This bizarre little company operates a full-service dinner train that provides a four-course meal along with two and a half hours of scenic train ride. Why would you want to eat dinner on a train? Well, looking at a constantly changing scenic view of Narragansett Bay is probably more interesting than your wallpaper. And if you have a fascination with interior decorating, you'll be glad to know that the railcars have all been restored to resemble the height of luxury car dining from long ago.

The company recently bought a pair of light railcars to use for their Touring Train, which will roll around Aquidneck Island. But the original Newport Dinner Train is the one still offering up their famous ribs, as well as chicken or fish. But since you call 1–800–398–RIBS in order to make your reservation, it's pretty obvious what entree you should order.

Carrier Pitchin'
Newport

The USS *Saratoga* Museum Foundation has done a lot of work. They have raised literally millions of dollars for the USS *Saratoga* Museum—and what better carrier to serve as a museum? There have been a half-dozen ships named *Saratoga*, but this USS *Saratoga* (the CV-60) was the second supercarrier in the world, a large Forrestal-class aircraft carrier. Built starting in 1952, the USS *Saratoga* was finally launched in 1955 and commissioned in 1956. It sailed to Guantanamo Bay in the 1950s, caught fire in the 1960s, and was deployed in the Pacific in the

1970s before being used as a staging area in the Vietnam War. Many aircraft flew from its deck, and the *Saratoga* received a battle star for its service. It was upgraded in the 1980s, and served in Desert Storm in the early 1990s.

A storied history. No, really, it is storied. It was in a Tom Clancy story called *Red Storm Rising* and was the ship that Captain Ron called "Good Ol' Sara," short for *Saratoga*. Hey, at least he didn't call it "Toga." It was also present for the Cuban Missile Crisis, the Six-Day War in the Middle East, and NATO operations in Bosnia. After an exciting life, the USS *Saratoga* was decommissioned in Florida in 1994, towed to Philadelphia in 1995, and finally moved to Newport in 1998. Now sitting in a Newport harbor, it was the perfect aircraft carrier to use as a museum.

But there was a snag: The U.S. Navy still owned the ship, and hadn't given it over to the foundation's care. So for roughly a decade it sat in Newport, no longer in service as a ship, but still not open to the public either. In fact, at the time of this writing in 2006, the USS *Saratoga* CV-60 is still not a museum. The *Saratoga* still sits in wait, more than 1,000 feet long and 250 feet wide, a massive floating monument that people can only view from the outside. However, the plans continue to convert the *Saratoga* into a museum in North Kingstown, and many donations have been gathered for that purpose. And as soon as the navy agrees, you'll be able to walk through the famed *Saratoga* as a museum. Meanwhile in Newport, it makes a lovely and extremely large dock ornament.

For more information visit www.saratogamuseum.org.

Music Forte
Newport

Fort Adams State Park on Brenton's Point has some of the best-kept athletic fields in New England, and also plays host to a number of jazz and folk concerts. Now this isn't necessarily odd for a state park, but Fort Adams State Park also contains Fort Adams, the largest coastal fortification in the country. So how did Newport's great fort go from military base to public space?

The question is, do you feel lucky, punk?

Glad you asked. The site on which Fort Adams was built was first used during the American Revolution in 1776, as an earthen fortification from which guns were fired at British warships. It was so successful that the British decided to burn it down three years later during their occupation. Nonetheless, the importance of a fortification on Brenton's Point was clear, and in 1799 the first Fort Adams (named for then-president John Adams) was built. After the War of 1812, although the fort didn't see very much action, it was decided that better coastal defenses were necessary, and so in 1824 construction began on the current Fort Adams.

It took thirty years to finish building, but it was garrisoned as early as 1841, because that's how war is. Once complete, the fort could hold 2,400 men and 468 cannons, though it was never filled with cannons to capacity, and it was never attacked—and good thing, because state-of-the-art granite walls from 1824 suddenly become rather pathetic in the face of twentieth-century shells and gunnery. Once airplanes were invented, the military utility of Fort Adams was all but finished. It was still used for training for a few years, and was finally deactivated in 1950.

Fort Adams was given to the U.S. Navy in 1953, which used it to house military families for a few years before finally turning it over to the State of Rhode Island for use as a state park in 1965. It has since been recognized as a National Historic Landmark, and a trust exists to maintain and restore the fort. Meanwhile, it remains open for tours where you can crawl through the tunnels and climb the bastions of the fort by day, and occasionally catch a music festival or Civil War reenactment.

Most of the music at Fort Adams seems to be either folk or jazz, which is a shame, because the "1812 Overture" would seem to be a much better fit. After all, they've already got plenty of cannons. For more information on Fort Adams, including tours, concerts, and other events, visit www.fortadams.org.

Statuesque
Newport

People usually come to Newport to see the big dots on the map that they've heard about, like the ocean and fancy mansions. But when you drive into Newport, one of the first things you'll see after crossing the bridge is a lot full of statues. Sure, it's not likely to be on any of the big tours, but there's just as much artwork here as there is in any mansion or museum, and that's without even counting all the stained glass inside.

Welcome to Aardvark Antiques.

Aardvark Antiques is owned by Arthur Grover, who began in Providence by collecting various architectural pieces. In 1969 he moved to Newport, and the business expanded. First it was mostly lights and mantles, but the inside of the shop has everything from windows and old stained glass to antique tea sets. And even if you have no interest in antiques, you can't help but be impressed by the plethora of statues. There are the typical Greco-Roman–inspired statues and fountains. There are statues of children. There are statues of animals from dolphins and tortoises to giraffes and even dragons. The sculptures are purchased from foundries all over the world, which is probably a lot of *aard vork*.

> There's a full house at Aardvark Antiques,
> Filled with dragons, and statues of Greeks,
> Windows made of stained glass,
> Many tchotchkes of brass;
> Enough stuff you should go take a peek!

"We really like unique stuff," says Jay Danella, the owner's stepson. Jay also works at the store with his brother Rocko, and is happy to tell you how much you can expect to pay for the shiny dragon you had your eye on. Sadly, shiny dragons don't come cheap. But there are still all sorts of other goodies. In addition to the statues and stained glass, there are gigantic hand-carved chairs in odd shapes and old front gates from mansions. Arthur "Aardvark" Grover likes to buy out full estates, because that's how some of the most interesting stuff is acquired. The bigger, the better. Demolitions often provide interesting doors, and churches can usually be counted on for some good stained-glass windows.

While Grover also makes kiddie bumper boats, the antiques shop is his main focus. He moved the shop to its current location at the turn of the millennium. And why did he call it Aardvark Antiques? Well, an aardvark pokes around and picks things to eat, just like Grover pokes around and picks antiques for the shop. So in a sense, he's an aardvark with a diet of stained-glass windows. And it means that he could bill himself as "Arthur the Aardvark," although he currently doesn't. But the main reason he named it Aardvark is because he wanted to be the first antiques shop listed when people went to the phone book.

Sure, they don't move, but it's faster than visiting the zoo.

Still, the statues make Aardvark Antiques much more than just another antiques shop. Even if it were named Zymurgy Antiques, it should still be high on your list.

Visit Aardvark Antiques at 9 JT Connell Highway, call them at (401) 849–7233, or check out their Web site at www.aardvarkantiques.com.

Touro Touro Touro
Newport

When it comes to religion, Rhode Island has a history of being a little bit offbeat. After all, the state was founded by Roger Williams when he was asked to leave the Puritan colony of Massachusetts. (Those people were seriously holier than thou.) Thus he founded Rhode Island with a strong belief in separation of church and state. And while today Rhode Island is the most Catholic state in America, it's also the home of the country's oldest Jewish synagogue: Touro Synagogue. And not just anywhere in Rhode Island, but in Newport, in a county with only a few hundred Jews. And if that still doesn't make Touro Synagogue seem unlikely enough, then consider that Touro is a Sephardic synagogue despite the fact that most of the members are Ashkenazi (European descent).

It all began back in 1658 when a few Jewish families came to Newport and founded a congregation named Yeshuat Israel (literally "Salvation of Israel"). The building has been at the same location ever since, but it wasn't until more than a hundred years later that it was properly dedicated. Isaac Touro came to Newport to serve as the congregation's cantor and rabbi, traveling all the way from Amsterdam. After such a long trip, you'd want to have a proper synagogue for the man, *wooden shoe?* So, five years after his arrival, the synagogue was dedicated in December 1763. It was designed by the famous architect Peter Harrison, and stands as a marvel of classic design.

Touro Synagogue was captured by the British during the Revolutionary War in 1776 and used as a hospital, which may not sound like a great fate for the building, but it prevented it from being burned. Still, the most famous thing about Touro is probably a letter in their possession from George Washington. In 1790 Moses Seixas, warden of Newport's congregation Yeshuat Israel, wrote a letter to George Washington in the hopes of confirming that the new government would allow the Jews their freedom of religion. Seixas wrote to say he saw the government as "one which to bigotry gives no sanction, to persecution no assistance," and blessed Washington.

God's original residence. Well, one of them.

Washington wrote back with his own blessings, and confirmed that his government would guarantee religious freedom by repeating Seixas's own words: "Happily the Government of the United States, which gives to bigotry no sanction, to persecution no assistance requires only that they who live under its protection should demean themselves as good citizens, in giving it on all occasions their effectual support."

If you want to hear the letter in its entirety, just show up at Touro Synagogue in August, where every year it is read aloud in a public cere-mony as part of a weekend celebration run by the Touro Synagogue Foundation.

Touro was named a National Historic Site in 1946 and became part of the National Trust for Historic Preservation in 2001. Touro is used for worship by the congregation, but they are proud stewards of this historical symbol of freedom, so you can take a tour of the synagogue, which is located at 85 Touro Street, most afternoons when it's not in use. If you would like more information, you can contact the Touro Synagogue Foundation at (401) 847–4794 or visit www.tourosynagogue .org.

OUTWIT, OUTLAST, OUTEVADE

In 2005 there was a man from Newport who was indicted for tax evasion. This in itself would not be too unusual, as tax evasion does occur regularly, in spite of being highly illegal. Usually the conceit behind tax evasion is that nobody else knows how much money you made, so they can't prove that you didn't pay taxes on it. In this man's case, however, there was a small snag: He had won a million dollars on national television.

Richard Hatch, a Newport native, was the winner of the very first season of the CBS reality series *Survivor*, back in 2000. At that point, he was thirty-nine years old and had had a wide range of careers. He had spent five years in the army and had worked as a bartender, car salesman, real estate agent, and most recently, corporate trainer. During the show, Hatch suggested that his experience as a corporate trainer had given him a valuable leg up on the other contestants. (Hatch also had a penchant for nudity.) And indeed, at the end of the season when everyone else had been voted off of the island, Richard Hatch emerged victorious, with a nice million-dollar prize to show for it.

Mysteriously, this million dollars never appeared on Hatch's 2000 tax return. And in 2005 the U.S. Attorney's office finally realized this. Hatch was charged with tax evasion on not only the million-dollar prize, but another $10,000 that CBS had paid him for a final appearance, as well as more than $300,000 that a radio station in Boston had paid him. Richard tried to hatch a plan to avoid trouble, but his appearances on national television may have worked against him. Not only had much of America seen that he had won the million dollars, but they'd also seen him try to manipulate people to win money.

Hatch originally had a deal to plead guilty in return for a more lenient sentence, but backed out of it and was indicted. In 2006 he was found guilty and sentenced to fifty-one months in jail. Perhaps his experience will come in handy as he embarks upon his new reality—*Survivor: Prison*.

Not Just Awful, Awful Awful
Newport

Language is an odd thing. Negative adjectives can become slang for positive, such as "bad" did a few decades ago. Rhode Islanders even now may call something "wicked" to mean that it is fantastic. But there is a dessert in Rhode Island that exemplifies this trend better than anything else: the Awful Awful. Some people will try to tell you that it's short for "Awful Big, Awful Good," and sure, that's what it says on the cups. But don't you believe them. That's just a slogan, and what you're drinking is simply an Awful Awful. Er . . . so what is it exactly?

Well, the Awful Awful is an ice-cream drink made by Newport Creamery. It's important not to call it a milk shake for two reasons. First, in Rhode Island, asking for a "milk shake" will get you a drink with milk. If you want the ice-cream drink that's often referred to as a milk shake elsewhere, in Rhode Island you have to order a "cabinet." But more importantly, the Awful Awful isn't even a cabinet. It's made with a special kind of ice milk mix, made only by Newport Creamery. They serve them in paper cups to go, but they taste better when you sit down inside to eat them. Because Newport Creamery is also a restaurant.

Sure, they didn't start as a restaurant. They started as a wholesale milk business back in 1928, with the one location in Newport. But in 1949 they built an ice-cream and food manufacturing plant, and started opening new locations. Newport Creameries began popping up across the state. And in addition to ice cream, patrons could also buy standard lunch items like burgers and sandwiches—and, of course, the Awful Awful. For some reason, it just tastes better when drunk out of the glass glass instead of the paper cup. But the real reason to drink an Awful Awful sitting in the restaurant is this: You can win a free one.

As far back as I can remember, Newport Creamery has had a standing offer: If you can order and drink three Awful Awfuls in one sitting, they'll give you a fourth one for free. Some restaurants have the occasional impossible eating contest like the five-pound steak, but Newport Creamery may be the only chain restaurant with not only a constant imbibing prize, but also a fairly manageable one. Hey, I've done it, and it was delicious, although I had brain freeze and ice-cream head afterwards like you wouldn't believe.

Sadly, at the turn of the millennium, the owners of Newport Creamery declared bankruptcy and closed a number of locations. But the business was then purchased by the Jan Companies, so there are still a dozen Newport Creameries you can visit to get some food. Or an Awful Awful. Or three. For a list of locations visit www.newportcreamery.com.

Awful Awfuls: Drink three, get one free. And a stomach ache.

Throwing Their Weight Around
Newport

If you want to see sumo wrestling, but don't have the time to fly all the way to Japan, you might appreciate Newport's annual Black Ships Festival. The festival, which takes place each July, celebrates Japanese culture in all forms, and one of the biggest forms of Japanese culture is the glorious tradition of sumo. Two very large men face off in a circle, and each tries to force the other to leave the circle or land on the ground. While it may sound simple, there are a number of complicated strategies and techniques, many of which are exhibited by the wrestlers with great skill. Even though the ring may be set up in the middle of a Newport thoroughfare instead of a Japanese stadium, the wrestlers are still high-caliber, some of them having retired from professional Japanese sumo.

They say the camera adds ten pounds. These guys had dozens of cameras pointed at them.

Of course, if big men wearing nothing but a silk band around their waist and groin frighten you, there are plenty of other Japanese cultural delights at Black Ships. Various other fighting styles and martial arts are demonstrated, both with weapons and without, though perhaps none so exciting as sumo. There are tea ceremonies and sushi to be eaten, though if you eat too much you may end up looking like a sumo wrestler. And perhaps most famously, the festival features taiko drumming, where traditional Japanese drums, including very large and rotund ones, are played by hitting them with great skill. But if you really want to see something large and rotund hit with great skill in a traditional Japanese manner, I still recommend sumo.

The name Black Ships comes from the Japanese term for foreign ships, which were not allowed into Japanese ports until Newport's Commodore Perry negotiated the historic Treaty of Kanagawa in 1854. Ever since then, the United States and Japan have been trading partners. The Black Ships Festival commemorates the treaty, as well as celebrating all the wonderful culture that Japan has to offer. Like sumo.

For more information visit http://www.newportevents.com/Black ships/main.shtml.

Mast Mass

Newport

If ships with big sails are cool (and they are), then ships with really big sails are really cool. And if you want to see many of the world's coolest ships all in one place, you really don't want to miss the Tall Ships festival in Newport. This festival often draws many of the world's tallest ships, from Russia to Germany to New Zealand to Brazil. How tall? Well, some of the masts are more than 150 feet high. In fact, the biggest Tall Ships boast sails with area that totals well over 20,000 square feet. It's no wonder that crowds of thousands gather at a port when even one of these ships is sailing in. Seeing a dozen at once is nothing less than stunning.

Of course, getting the world's tallest ships all in one place isn't easy, which is why the Tall Ships festival does not come to Newport every year. In July 2006 just the USCGC *Eagle* (known as "America's Tall Ship") came to town for a change-of-command ceremony. But in July 2007 two dozen ships are slated to sail into Newport. In addition to marveling at the glory of ships more than 300 feet long, people are encouraged to invite crew members to conversation or even dinner (which would likely include conversation, because people who have sailed from another country usually have a lot to talk about). And some lucky young folks can even sign up to help crew the ships as part of a training program.

Even if you don't help run a ship or chat with the people who do, it's worth keeping track of when the Tall Ships will next be passing through Newport so you can see them, which given their size, really isn't hard if you're anywhere close. It's not a mast to be missed. For more information go to www.tallshipsrhodeisland.org.

That's Your Theory

Newport

The Old Stone Mill is definitely one of Rhode Island's great historical buildings. Also known as the Viking Stone Mill or Norse Tower, this giant cylindrical stone building stands in Touro Park in Newport. The tower is 24 feet high, with arches on the bottom and square holes on the top. The construction has largely withstood the test of time, and the tower is a beautiful sight to behold, clearly a relic of a previous age. And perhaps the most salient feature of this "Mystery Tower" is this: Nobody knows where the heck it came from.

However, there are plenty of guesses. Some say that the tower was built by the Vikings a millennium ago. Some of the ancient Norse sagas have made vague references to an area that could well have been New England. And there is some evidence to suggest that the tower may have been a Viking church. Not only does the shape of the building itself resemble the early church buildings in Scandinavia, but the Viking Stone Mill also happens to be perfectly oriented to the points of the compass, as were all Scandinavian churches at that time.

"It's colonial English," Bob thought.
"No, an old Viking tower," said Scott.
I said, "Guys, there must be
Things on which you agree?"
"Yes there are: We agree we do not."

Then again, it could have been built by colonial settlers. Governor Benedict Arnold, the great-grandfather of the more infamous Benedict Arnold, left a will upon his death in 1677 that referred to a "stone built windmill," which he is said to have constructed. And the Old Stone Mill does resemble the mills of England, where Arnold was born. In 1848 the mortar of various city buildings, including Governor Arnold's tomb and a stone house

The Old Stone Mill: We're not sure how it got there, but we're glad to have it just the same.

on Spring Street dating from 1639, were compared to mortar from the tower and found to be "identical in quality and character."

Viking-theory supporters insist that while Governor Arnold may have converted this building into a windmill, it was still initially constructed by the Vikings in their colony called "Vinland." After all, why else would Longfellow have written a poem ("The Skeleton in Armor") about a Viking who sailed to Vinland to build a stone tower for his beloved? Unfortunately, the Viking theory has lost some credence since carbon-14 dating samples have pegged the mortar as no older than the fifteenth century.

Still, that doesn't mean that colonials necessarily built it. Some have argued that the tower is actually a combination church and fortified watchtower, built by Portuguese explorers, since the stonework is very similar to other Portuguese structures of the time. Still others argue that it was built by the Chinese as a device for determining longitude, or the Indians who were native to the land, or the Knights Templar after the Crusades, or even the ancient druids (who have a history of leaving mysterious stone buildings around).

While wild speculation continues to this day, the current reigning theory is that of the colonials. An archaeological dig uncovered grinding stones that supported the gristmill theory, as well as a footprint that seems to have been made by a colonial shoe. For this reason, the plaque now at the tower reads as follows: OLD STONE MILL / BUILT PROBABLY ABOUT 1660 / BY BENEDICT ARNOLD / FIRST GOVERNOR OF RHODE ISLAND / UNDER THE CHARTER OF 1643 / REFERRED TO IN HIS WILL AS / "MY STONE BUILT WINDMILL" / LEGEND ASCRIBED ITS ERECTION TO THE / NORSEMEN DURING THEIR SUPPOSED / VISIT ABOUT 1000 A.D.

But if it was really built by the colonial English instead of Vikings, why do none of the measurements line up with any English measurements? Perhaps you'll have to go investigate and find out for yourself.

Touro Park is on Bellvue Avenue in the center of Newport.

Unpetrified Wood
Newport

A cursory glance at the famed Redwood Library & Athenaeum of Newport would show it to be made of stone, just as you'd expect from a building that has been around since the eighteenth century. And that cursory glance would be more wrong than putting tomatoes in clam chowder. Because the Redwood Library is—surprise!—made of wood. The wooden planks are carved to give the appearance of stone, thanks to the genius of architect Peter Harrison. Of course, he could have never predicted that 250 years later, people would be coloring plastic to give the appearance of wood.

But Harrison was old school even for the eighteenth century. He based his plan for the Redwood Library & Athenaeum on an old drawing of a Roman temple, complete with portico and wings. And some-

Looks like stone, doesn't it?

how, based only on a small two-dimensional drawing, he managed to create a fairly convincing building. Sure, he didn't have a surplus of stone and slaves, so the building's actually made of wood, but it still manages to impress. In fact, the Roman temple–inspired architecture can probably be blamed for most of America's government buildings today. After visiting the Redwood Library back in 1790, Thomas Jefferson decided that public buildings should have classical architecture. At least he didn't demand that they all be made of wood.

Did I mention that the library is old? It's really, really old. In fact, it's the oldest lending library in America, as well as the oldest library building in continuous use, having been lending out books since 1750. Why the first? Well, it didn't have to wait for public support. Unlike most libraries which are supported by tax, Redwood is an independent subscription library supported by membership fees and gifts. It was founded back in 1747 by a group of people who, according to their charter, had "nothing in view but the good of mankind," hence the reason why it's an athenaeum for learning as well as a library. And while there are membership fees, qualified scholars and researchers can still use the library without being members—though suspicion may be cast on any British officers.

You see, during the Revolutionary War, the library was taken over for use as a British officers' club, and more than half of the books disappeared from the shelves. The library has been trying to get them back since 1806, and they've done a pretty good job of it. Today the Redwood Library has reclaimed roughly 90 percent of the volumes that were lost, with more than 160,000 in its collection. The First Lady herself, Laura Bush, chaired their 2006 celebration. For those not interested in book-learnin', the library also has museum collections ranging from seventeenth-century portraiture to eighteenth-century furniture. And if that doesn't interest you either, then go back outside and marvel at the stone—I mean, wood.

The Redwood Library & Athenaeum is located at 50 Bellevue
Avenue, Newport. For more information call (401) 847–0292 or visit
www.redwoodlibrary.org.

Tennis, Anyone?
Newport

When most people think of tennis, the place that comes to mind is
Wimbledon. But the place that should come to mind is Newport. After
all, it is Newport that houses the International Tennis Hall of Fame, at
194 Bellevue Avenue (401–849–3990; www.tennisfame.com). For

The grass is always greener on the other side of the net.

something called the Hall of Fame, surprisingly few people know about it, but it was the site of the first U.S. National Championships in 1881, and continued to be until 1915.

The Hall of Fame was founded by James Van Allen, who invented a tie-breaking system for tennis, but did not invent any belts. In addition to the questionably famous hall itself, the complex also boasts the world's largest tennis museum, containing the world's largest collection of tennis memorabilia. And if that wasn't enough reason to visit, you can step onto a grass court yourself and have a few swings. The competition grass courts have been in continual use since the nineteenth century, and are open to the public for play.

Just don't expect to be able to use them without some negotiating up front. It's that kind of racquet.

Old-Style Tavern
Newport

If you're looking for a good old tavern, you won't find one older than the White Horse Tavern in Newport. It opened back in 1687 and is believed to be the oldest operating tavern in the country. It began as the meeting place for the colony's general assembly and city council, because even in the seventeenth century, politicians wanted good food that they could charge to the public. Aside from good food, the tavern was known for being owned by William Mayes, the famous pirate. His father owned the tavern before him, but it was the young Mayes who got the liquor license in 1702. (Perhaps a thirst for more rum?)

A few decades later, Jonathan Nichols took over as innkeeper and named the tavern the White Horse. It was converted to a boarding-house in 1901, but the Preservation Society of Newport County acquired it in 1954. Three years later it was restored and opened as a restaurant, which it has continued to be to this day. The colonial charm of beam ceilings and plank floors adds ambience to the food, which tends to center around local seafood. The food is delicious, but pricey, so diners concerned about cost should consider ordering from the Tavern menu, which is slightly cheaper. Reservations and appropriate attire are both recommended.

There are also a number of ghost stories involving the White Horse Tavern, but most of them seem to have happened years ago, so the only spirits with your meal should be in a glass. Just realize that if you are hearing voices, there's a chance it's not the wine.

The White Horse Tavern can be found at 26 Marlborough Street in Newport. Call (401) 849–3600 or visit www.whitehorsetavern.com for more information.

Plant or Animal?

Portsmouth

So you're all set to do something fun on a lovely summer day, but can't decide whether to see the animals at the zoo or the beautiful gardens that are growing. Why not split the difference and head down to Green Animals in Portsmouth?

Green Animals is the oldest topiary garden in the United States, containing twenty-one topiary animals and fifty-nine other topiaries of various objects. Granted, the animals may not move around as much as those at the zoo, but if you take your glasses off and squint, you won't be able to tell the difference. Besides, you can see much more interesting wildlife at the topiary garden than at the zoo. You can find an elephant in either place, but how many zoos have you been to that have a unicorn? Yeah, I thought so.

The estate that houses Green Animals once belonged to Thomas Brayton, who was the treasurer for the Union Cotton Manufacturing Company in Fall River. Brayton bought the estate in 1872 and, soon after, commissioned Portuguese gardener Joseph Carreiro (aka "Dahlia Joe") to bring the gardens to life. And he certainly did, crafting topiaries from yew, California privet, and English boxwood trees. In addition to the more common animals like camels and giraffes, and less common ones like the Rhode Island Red rooster and the teddy bear, there are topiaries in various geometric shapes, and even one of a policeman.

Brayton died in 1939, and Carreiro soon after in 1945. But Brayton had a daughter named Alice, who gave her father's estate the name Green Animals before inheriting it, and Carreiro had a son-in-law named George Mendonca, who took over the gardener's former position. Alice and George continued to maintain the gardens for decades, and Alice willed the estate to the Preservation Society of Newport County, which has been preserving it faithfully since her death in 1972.

If you want to hedge your bets, there's more than just topiary on the seven-acre estate. Head gardener James Donahue and his staff meticulously maintain not only the topiary, but also a rose garden, a dahlia bed (favorite of original gardener Joe Carreiro), fruit trees, a formal garden, and much more. Should you want to get out of the sun for a bit, the Victorian Brayton House contains a toy and doll museum. And who could resist the summer house built by Thomas Brayton back in 1880? Sure, it's not as exciting as the topiary, but it's a good place to rest if you're bushed.

Green Animals is open daily and admission is charged, except for children five and under, provided they don't try to ride the animals. It's located at 380 Cory's Lane, Portsmouth, and the telephone number is (401) 683-1267.

The Price of Prudence

Prudence Island

Prudence Island is a great place not to visit. Unlike most towns that would gladly dance the Watusi if it would bring them more tourist dollars, the 150 full-time residents of Prudence Island are very happy not to have many tourists. One sign of this is the conspicuous absence of hotels, bars, or even restaurants. Even so, the 5.5-square-mile island becomes somewhat populated in the summer, as nature lovers and boat lovers gravitate toward it and occasionally stay for the season.

Still, for most of the year, Prudence Island is a quiet, small, insular community. And that's just how the residents like it. They discourage commercial development on one-third of the island, and the other two-thirds don't allow development at all, which is why there is so much nature around. Residents not only have to like nature, but each other, because when you're the only 150 people on an island, you get pretty close. There is all of one school on the island, one year-round store, and very little in the way of entertainment aside from other residents.

But that's good, if you're a resident trying to find a place for community. Locals help each other out, talk with each other a lot, and have the occasional movie night and potluck dinner. They have a few community activities, appreciate the local nature, and generally enjoy a laid-back existence without the hubbub of a city around them. They can always take a ferry or water taxi to the mainland when they need something, but most residents enjoy the quiet privacy of the island; otherwise, they wouldn't live there.

Meanwhile, you can show up during hunting season or in the summer, but otherwise you'd probably do well to avoid Prudence Island. The residents have put up a Web site, www.prudenceisland.us, but even that is really for their convenience, and not yours. In short, you might describe Prudence Island like this: "A nice place to live, but I wouldn't want to visit there."

FASHION POLICE

Some women just love a man in uniform. And few men in uniform look better than the Rhode Island State Police. It may be hard to appreciate if you're only seeing them when they're giving you a speeding ticket, but their distinctive uniforms have earned them fame from coast to coast. Maybe it's the smart-looking boots. Maybe it's the bumps on the side of the legs. Or maybe it's the dapper hats. But whatever it is, the uniforms are some of the best in the country. That's why the RI State Police are generally favorites at the annual awards given by the National Association of Uniform Manufacturers and Distributors (NAUMD).

The NAUMD judges police uniforms from every state on overall appearance, neatness, projection of authority, practicality for designated functions, and adherence to uniform regulations. And Rhode Island is one of the main contenders, having won an Outstanding Achievement Award in 2004 for Best Dressed State Agency and a special Commemorative Award in 2006. Heck, Ohio was thrilled to tie with Rhode Island for first place back in 1986.

The fashionable Rhode Island state trooper uniforms have shown up in a few Hollywood movies, as well as some local cartoons. But most importantly, they continue to show up on the police around Rhode Island. Because if you're going to get pulled over, you may as well have something nice to look at.

Trooper Ernest McKenney of 161, looking fashionably serious.

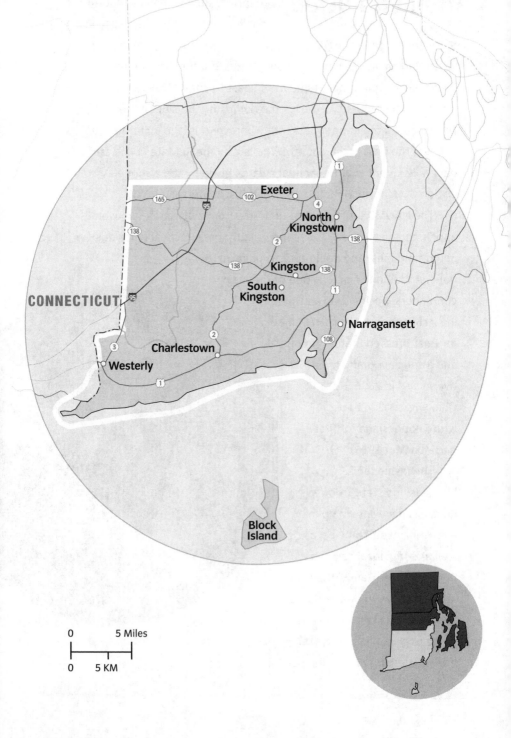

WASHINGTON COUNTY

WASHINGTON COUNTY

A Beacon of History
Block Island

No, it's not part of New York. Block Island is part of Rhode Island, and is surrounded by dangerous shoals. How dangerous? Well, dangerous enough to cause so many shipwrecks that in the nineteenth century, people called it the "stumbling block" of the coast. Clearly, a lighthouse was necessary, and after the northern lighthouse was built in 1829, there was a federal Grant to build the Southeast Light in 1875. And by federal Grant, we're talking about President Ulysses S., who had signed the appropriation order to have the lighthouse built.

Since it was essential to navigation through dangerous shores, the lighthouse was built with the most powerful lens available at the time: a first-order Fresnel lens costing $10,000 (that's 200 bills with Grant's picture on them). This was tacked on to a 52-foot-high Victorian Gothic station to become the tallest light on the New England coast. Grant himself even came down to visit.

In 1928 the station was electrified. Ten years later it was temporarily un-electrified when a big hurricane took its toll on the lighthouse. In addition to the destruction of the oil house, radio beacon, and numerous windows, all the power went out. But with such dangerous shoals off the coast, the Southeast Light could not rest, so the lighthouse keepers turned the lens by hand until power could be restored.

Back when the lighthouse was built in 1875, it was a full 300 feet away from the Mohegan Bluffs. But by 1990 the bluff looked like it was going to be called. The lighthouse was only 55 feet from the edge of the ever-eroding bluff, and the Coast Guard decided to deactivate it and replace it with a steel tower and automated signal beacon. But the historic lighthouse had its fans, who couldn't bear to see it destroyed. A group of volunteers called the Block Island Southeast Lighthouse Foundation raised $2 million to pay for the lighthouse to be relocated 300 feet away from the new edge of the cliffs.

In 1993 it was time to move the lighthouse. Moving a lighthouse is a lot like moving a bookcase, presuming your bookcase is 52 feet tall and weighs four million pounds. Actually, come to think of it, it's very different than moving a bookcase. The Army Corps of Engineers used thirty-eight hydraulic lifts and countless tons of steel rails and cable, and within a few months actually managed to move the lighthouse to a new location 300 feet from the edge of the cliff. The Southeast Light was reactivated from its new location a year later.

Let's just hope they don't have to move it again in another hundred years. But just in case, you should go visit it now. There are only a dozen working first-order Fresnel lenses in the country, and this one is valued at $3 million (which is 60,000 bills with Grant's picture on them, if you're still keeping track). Four people can stand inside the lens, which flashes green every five seconds. Tours of the tower are offered in the summer, and numerous ferry boats go to the island.

To get more information about tours, or chat about the glory of Fresnel lenses, call the Block Island Southeast Lighthouse Foundation at (401) 466–5009. You can also visit the Web site at http://lighthouse.cc/blockisoutheast.

Good Old-Fashioned Powwow
Charlestown

The Narragansett Indians know how to party. And they know how to have a meeting. The secret to both? Doing them at once. The Narragansett Annual Meeting, aka the Narragansett Powwow, has been running annually for more than 330 years and is the oldest powwow in the country. In fact, the word *powwow* itself is derived from the Narragansett *powwaw*, which means "spiritual leader." Nowadays a powwow describes any of the big meetings that Native American tribes might have, when they join together for traditional singing and dancing. Powwows generally start with a grand entry, where everyone in the ceremony files in before they get down to singing and dancing.

The Narragansett Powwow in Charlestown follows that tradition because, heck, it *is* the tradition. But when you're the oldest powwow in the country, it might be more accurate to say that tradition follows you. The Narragansetts' current medicine man is named Running Wolf, who gave a blessing to open the 331st annual powwow on August 12, 2006. Drums and chanting then picked up for the grand entry, where dozens and dozens of Narragansetts in traditional dress proceeded in the procession. And in case you aren't familiar with traditional Narragansett dress, that means the women wore long skirts, jewelry, and a few feathers in their hair, and the men had colorful outfits with bright vests, jewelry, and lots and lots of feathers. Yes, Indians do actually dress like that—but just for ceremonies, not every day, unless they're in a movie.

Anyway, the annual Narragansett Powwow has a bit of serious business, like the song of honor, the cleansing of the circle, presentation of the peace pipe, and prayer. After that, there's some serious fun in the form of traditional singing and dancing, which, though entertaining to watch, they actually take quite seriously. And then there's the fun fun, with children dancing, food, and vendors of all sorts of traditional Native American crafts. You can bet on finding some turquoise at any powwow. And speaking of betting, one of the big issues at the powwow of late has been the proposed casino for the Narragansetts in Rhode Island. The casino has many opponents, but most of the Narragansetts are hoping to *whomp 'em.*

For more information visit www.narragansett-tribe.org.

A Relish for Relics
Exeter

In the past five years Hubert "Hub" Dyer of Exeter has renovated his shed and filled it up with a plethora of collectable items. A .30 Winchester rifle he once hunted with. A sword. Belt buckles and Indian paintings. But his real prize is his collection of arrowheads. He began collecting when he was only nine years old, and has amassed an impressive array of arrowheads, spearheads, knife blades, and ax heads. How can he tell an arrowhead from a spearhead from a knife blade? Arrowheads have to be made from very thin and light rocks, so as not to throw off the balance of the arrow, while spearheads are more elongated while still light, and knives are larger.

But more importantly, how can you tell an arrowhead or other Indian artifact from another rock on the ground? Well, chances are, you can't. Hub can, and that's why he keeps finding arrowheads and you don't. "It's an inner knowledge you can't explain; you somehow know what you're looking for. You have to have a feeling for it."

The one thing he will say about finding Indian artifacts is that frost brings them up and rain washes them out. "But you need the eye," says Hub, crediting his successful finds to his instinct. "God gave me a gift—Indian knowledge." His great-grandmother was Native American, so that may help with his instincts. And when instincts aren't enough, he also has a collection of books about Indians. But a shelf full of books is not the same as a shelf full of arrowheads that you've found, so one has to agree when Hub claims he has a gift for it.

He's found pieces from every corner of Rhode Island, from South Kingston to Johnston to Alton Jones. Once while digging a hole to make a campfire while serving as a scoutmaster, he found some coals that he could tell were from an ancient campfire, so he kept digging until a foot and a half down, he found some relics from the Narra-gansett massacre on

Hub Dyer is a man who knows his arrowheads. Each and every one.

Swampfight Island—including an intact medicine man's pipe. Put that in *your* pipe and smoke it. Hub can spot an atlatl weight from 50 feet away, and can tell at a glance if a rock was once an ax head and whether it was from a standard ax or an ax blade held directly in the hand. The latter are more groovey (literally—they have grooves where the fingers wore the rock away).

For many years Hub worked at Mount Yawgoo, where he laid out some ski trails. The last one he did, back in 1966, was even named for him: Hub's Folly. But it's hardly folly when he continues to find pestles and adzes just by walking those trails. "You can find artifacts on any woods trail, if you have the eye," explains Hub, noting that most people may well kick an arrowhead out of their way and never know it. But until other local people with the eye start grabbing arrowheads, Hub will continue touring schools in the area to show off his collection. After all, he's an arrowheadhead.

Have Mercy!

Exeter

If one of your family members was sick with tuberculosis, what would you think is the most likely cause? If you answered, "A vampiric other family member returning from the dead to drain their lifeforce," then you got the same answer that George T. Brown came up with in the 1890s. His wife, Mary, died in 1883 and his eldest daughter, Mary Olive, died a few years later. In 1892 his other daughter, Mercy, died and his son, Edwin, became sick. George T. Brown, as any good father would, wanted to find a cure.

Medical science in the 1890s wasn't quite as advanced as it is today, and superstition reigned supreme. George believed one of his dead family members was returning as a vampire to cause Edwin's illness, and got people to help him exhume the bodies of his family for examination. Sure enough, Mercy's body was not nearly as decomposed as that of her mother or sister, which was clearly because she was a vampire and not at all related to the fact that she had only been dead a few months instead of four years. Her chest was cut open and liquid blood was found in her heart, which was taken as the final proof needed that Mercy Brown was a vampire and the cause of the tuberculosis—not only in Edwin, but in other sick people in the community as well.

The grave of Mercy Brown, vampire. Hopefully she's dead . . .

227

Long ago, people made the assumption
That a vampire was causing consumption.
So her heart was exhumed,
And by flames was consumed,
Which I'd guess took a whole lot of gumption.

Naturally, once you've found the heart of a tuberculosis-causing vampire, you have to burn it. The *Providence Journal*, a very forward-thinking newspaper, had an editorial at the time condemning the practice of exhuming bodies to burn their hearts. But George was undeterred, and after burning Mercy's heart, mixed the ashes with water to make a drink for Edwin. Nineteenth-century lore said that drinking the vampire's heart would remove the curse. Modern science says eating dead people isn't too healthy, and indeed Edwin died soon after.

Nonetheless, Mercy Brown remains as one of the most famous non-Transylvanian vampires ever. Her gravestone is in the Chestnut Hill Cemetery behind the Chestnut Hill Baptist Church on Route 102 in Exeter.

Some say that Mercy Brown still walks through the graveyard—watching, waiting, and sometimes whispering or whimpering. Also watching and waiting is Mercy's descendent Lewis Peck, especially around Halloween, to deter anyone who would vandalize the grave site. So between the vampire ghost and the vampire heir, we recommend that if you do visit the grave of Mercy Brown, be respectful. Nobody wants an angry vampire.

Not Just Jocks

Kingston

The World Scholar-Athlete Games in Rhode Island are probably not what you'd expect from an international sports event. The fifteen-to-nineteen-year-old students who participate have to possess fairly high academic achievement in addition to their skill in sports, hence the scholar part of the title. Every four years or so, more than 1,500 of these scholars from all over the world come to Rhode Island to compete in well over a dozen different sports and participate in about half as many cultural events. That's right, cultural events. While many of the students are athletes skilled at a particular sport, some of the participants come to show off their talents in the arts instead (apparently "World Scholar-Athlete-Artist Games" wouldn't fit on their postcards).

But perhaps the most unconventional part of this competition is the way the teams work. Rather than living and competing with your team of, say, seven people from Colombia, each person is assigned a random roommate when they arrive and will later be put on a diverse team consisting of people they've never met before, generally from different countries. So rather than playing with the few local friends they've practiced with, a soccer team might consist of sixteen people from thirteen different countries. And while calling complicated plays in four languages might be tricky, everyone understands the concept of "Get the ball over there." Students are quick to make friends with other students from countries ranging from Antigua to Zambia, in a manner that most ambassadors and diplomats might envy.

Such is the power of sports diplomacy. Many believe that Ping-Pong is what connected us with China, and now the hope is that the World Scholar-Athlete Games will foster more international communication and understanding between students of different countries. The games are sponsored by the Institute for International Sport in Kingston, which was founded by Daniel Doyle in 1986. Doyle took his basketball team to Cuba in 1980, and after connecting with the people there in spite of political disagreement, decided that the best way to communicate with the world was sports.

However, once you've got a bunch of scholars together by tempting them with sports, you can start throwing international issues at them. Each year the Scholar-Athlete Games focuses on a few important international issues like global environment or world peace—you know, good stuff for kids. Various speakers ranging from Bill O'Reilly to Bill Clinton to Bill Bradley have come to talk to the students about these topics and lead them in discussions. Sometimes the speakers aren't even named Bill. So far the games have occurred four times: in 1993, 1997, 2001, and 2006. 2006's games had roughly 1,900 students representing 155 different countries.

If nothing else, they've certainly been more effective than our country's recent foreign policy in terms of promoting international friendships. If you'd like more information about the program, or if you know of a scholar-athlete you'd like to nominate for the games, you can write to Megan Hinners, 3045 Kingstown Road, P.O. Box 1710, Kingston, RI 02881, or go their Web site at www.internationalsport.com. Just be warned, accepted students still have to pay more than $500 for the program.

Happy As a Clam
Narragansett

Since Rhode Island is the Ocean State, it makes sense that Rhode Islanders put a high importance on their seafood. And one of everyone's favorite places to get fresh-fried seafood each summer is Aunt Carrie's (401–783–7930), in Narragansett.

Aunt Carrie's is a Rhode Island institution, having been around since 1920. It all began with Carrie Cooper, whose husband bemoaned the lack of cold drinks available around Narragansett. She did what any dutiful 1920s wife would do—she started making lemonade.

In fact, she ended up making a little restaurant on the beach to sell the lemonade. Due to the location, kids kept bringing up clams from the beach, and she would make them into chowder and clam cakes. Eventually, she realized that people were more interested in her clam cakes

She sells seafood by the seashore.

and chowder than they were in her lemonade, so she began selling them. Due to Cooper's many nieces and nephews, everyone called her "Aunt Carrie," and thus came the famous name. Carrie Cooper died in 1964, and Aunt Carrie's was taken over by her daughter Gertrude and grandchild Bill, as well as Bill's wife, Elsie, in 1984. By 1994 it was just Elsie Foy, who currently runs the restaurant with her two daughters, fourth-generation children of the original Aunt Carrie.

Of course, most people who eat at Aunt Carrie's don't know about the particular history, and don't necessarily care. What they do care about is that Aunt Carrie's has been around longer than they've been alive and serves up fried clams, clam cakes, clam chowder, and shore dinners, right on the ocean, every summer. Some people prefer going inside for the full dinner, including all three forms of clams, fish, french fries, lobster, and dessert. (Aunt Carrie's is well-known for their wonderful rhubarb pie.) Others, like myself, prefer to grab a plate of fried clams and then sit outside to enjoy the ocean air.

Regardless of where you eat your clams, Rhode Islanders agree that summer isn't summer without Aunt Carrie's. And conversely, when it isn't summer there isn't Aunt Carrie's, so don't try to visit during the off-season or it will be closed. But show up at 1240 Ocean Road on a weekend in April, May, and September, or any day except Tuesday from June through August, and the fresh seafood will leave you *Carrie'd* away.

SWAMPED WITH BLOOD

Narragansett is a town in Rhode Island, and like many towns in Rhode Island, it was originally the name of an Indian tribe that lived on this land before it was ever Rhode Island.

The Narragansett was a fairly powerful tribe back in the late seventeenth century, known as warriors who could help protect some of the weaker local tribes. Still, they were living peacefully in the same general area as Roger Williams and his band of non-Puritan colonials, who had gotten the Narragansetts to let them use some land in Providence. But as usual, peace was only temporary.

In 1675 King Philip and his Wampanoag tribe tried to reclaim some land for the Indians. And while the Narragansett tribe was theoretically neutral, things were a wigwam, things were a teepee, things were a wigwam, things were a teepee—in short, things were too tense. The colonists were afraid that the battle-ready Narragansett would join the Wampanoag and take back colonial land for the Indians in a bloody battle. So the colonists decided to launch a preemptive strike. Josiah Winslow led a small force from Plymouth (yes, the place with the rock) to attack the Narragansett in November, and on December 19, 1675, the real massacre happened. An Indian informant had told the colonists about a Narragansett winter camp, so General Winslow and famed Indian fighter Benjamin Church helped gather a large force of Puritans and Puritan sympathizers, and stormed the winter camp with well over a thousand men.

The result became known as the Great Swamp Massacre. Most of the Narragansett in the winter camp were women, children, and old people, so once the colonials breached the camp, it fell quickly. Estimates of the Indians killed on that day range from 300 to more

CONTINUED

than 500, with very few of them warriors, for the warriors had mostly escaped into the swamp.

As you might expect, the remaining Narragansett warriors were angry. With their home destroyed, they broke their neutral stance and joined King Philip and the Wampanoags. A few months later, in March 1676, Warwick was attacked. A party of Narragansetts even burned down most of the houses in Providence, including that of Roger Williams. The peace that had reigned was destroyed.

Centuries later the Great Swamp Massacre is still remembered. The current Narragansett Reservation occupies some of the same territory as the swamps, and there is even a statue of the old Narragansett leader from 1675. The tribe holds an annual ceremony to commemorate the anniversary of the event. But some say that the spirits of the dead remain restless, and that if you walk through that Indian burial ground at night, you can still hear the screams of the Indian women being slaughtered. It's not a particularly cheerful piece of history, but that's why it's called the Great Swamp Massacre instead of Colonial Funfest.

The Two Towers
Narragansett

Not the Lord of the Rings, but the Lords of the Bling would gather at the famous Narragansett Pier Casino back in the 1890s. Seriously, if you had the money for an extravagant vacation back at the end of the nineteenth century, there were few better places to go than Narragansett. And the glorious towers served as a gateway to the best place to hang out for a few weeks, with nearly twenty major luxury hotels all in the same place, around a casino that offered not only cards and billiards, but also bowling, tennis, boating, shooting, and various other games and sports. This was important, because since cars weren't really around, you needed your hotel to be within a short distance of big fun.

And the Towers, which still stretch across Ocean Drive, were a centerpiece of that resort hotspot. Designed by McKim, Mead & White, construction on the Towers began in 1883 and finished in 1886. Almost

The Towers of Power. Gateway to the world. Go through, there's the world.

immediately after that, Narragansett became *the* place to go. In addition to all the aforementioned entertainment options, the Narragansett Pier offered restaurants, stores, a ballroom, a bandstand, and even a theater. People would come to bathe at the beach, dance at one of the evening hops, or take a leisurely promenade across the arch of the Towers themselves. And if all this wasn't enough excitement, the superrich used the Towers as a literal gateway to their final destination of Newport's mansions. Arriving by train from New York and Boston, the superrich stopped in at the Pier Casino before boating on to Vanderbilt galas, while the merely moderately rich stayed at the casino to watch horse racing and play polo.

Unfortunately, like another set of towers, disaster struck—and eerily around the same time. On September 12, 1900, a huge fire broke out in the Rockingham Hotel. It soon spread across the street to the Pier Casino, and a few hours later, most of the casino had burned to the ground. Only the stone walls of the Towers were left standing. But Narragansett would not be deterred. A new casino, with the same designers, was opened on July 8, 1905, with the new, renovated Towers finished in 1910. They stood strong against the hurricanes of 1938 and 1954, before being severely damaged by another fire in 1965. Still, they managed to survive the hurricane of 1991, and gained a legendary reputation for standing tall while surrounding buildings were literally blown away.

Such a historic building couldn't be allowed to disappear, so Narragansett has restored the Towers, including a porch overlooking the ocean. It functions today as a venue for everything from jazz concerts to fashion shows. Heck, I even once attended a wedding there. If you're going to Narragansett, you really can't miss it, but in case you want more information, the phone number is (401) 782–2597 and the Web site, www.thetowersri.com.

Rune with a View

North Kingstown

Rune-reader Victoria Clare spent a year living in Norway from 2002 to 2003, and looks back on her time with no remorse. She does, however, look back with re-Norse, because it is the Norse culture and religious connections that she picked up while in Norway. Clare had always been interested in the Norse gods, which is why she was willing to sell pretty much everything she owned in order to journey to Norway. Asatru fact. Asatru literally means "belief in the gods," and is the name of the Norse Heathen religion, as well as those who practice it.

A handful of Norse runes.

When Clare embraced Asatru, she got in touch with the Norns, the wise women who control fate, and learned to consult Urd, Verdandi, and Skuld to understand the past and future. But you can't call the three fates on the telephone to consult them, so Clare learned to cast runes. As an added bonus, says Clare, runes can be used to bind your enemies or heal wounds, since after tapping into the energy, much can be done with a chant. However, she uses them primarily for divination.

Clare was accepted by the Asatru clergy to have a kindred, and is now the spiritual leader of a group called the Osprey Kindred. She is a member of the Rune Gild, and feels that most people misunderstand rune-reading. First of all, the majority of individuals who tell fortunes these days tend to use Tarot cards, not runes. But those who do use runes tend to use a Buddhist book, while she bases her rune reading on the lore-based writings of Tacitus. She sits on a three-legged stool, faces north, says a sacred verse, chants, and then casts the Elder Futhark (which is not her grandpa, but the name of the set of twenty-four Norse runes), all carved on chips of wood.

Of course, since rune-reading is not a commonly desired commodity, she only shows up for open rune-reading hours every few Saturday afternoons at the Herb Wyfe in Wickford, North Kingstown (401–295–1140; www.herbwyfe.com). By day, she works in a law firm. But this is not to imply she doesn't have runes in her daily life. She casts runes every day to meditate, calling on Odin to open her eyes to the future. But if you'd like her future to include doing a rune reading for you, you can call to set up an appointment at (401) 667–7229 or e-mail her at snillgaupe@cox.net (Snillgaupe is her Norse nickname, meaning "nice bobcat").

And don't be afraid to do some research before you contact her. Clare says too many people reading runes today haven't studied them, which really maketh her Thor.

Build and Sting

North Kingstown

At first glance, when you see a bee with a sailor hat holding a wrench and a machine gun, you might be tempted to say that although it does make for a very cool statue, it doesn't make much sense. But the Seabees are the U.S. Navy's construction battalion, and the two things they're good at are building and fighting. Just like bees! But bees also make honey, which the Seabees do not do, which is why the guns and wrenches are there for emphasis and clarification.

Anyway, the Seabees were born in Rhode Island at the start of World War II. Originally, the navy just used soldiers for fighting and civilians to build things, like bases on various Pacific Islands. But since things were being built in the middle of a war, civilian construction crews were in a bad situation when enemy forces came to destroy their work. International law declared that civilians couldn't be armed and resist enemy forces, or they could be executed as guerrillas. So the construction crew building the base on Wake Island had no protection when the Japanese came and killed some of them and took the rest of them prisoner, forcing them into years of labor and eventually executing them anyway.

This brought home the idea that Americans building bases also needed to be soldiers. And so in January 1942 the First Construction Detachment left from Quonset Point in Rhode Island. Once it had gathered nearly 300 men from a few other locations, it was deployed to build a fuel tank farm in Bora Bora. In September of that year, the Seabees went to Guadalcanal for their first work in a combat zone, building an airfield under heavy fire from both the Japanese and the weather. After that the Seabees were at the forefront of every island invasion in the Pacific, paving the way—literally—for the troops that would follow. The secret of their success? Experience. While most soldiers were young men barely out of their teens, the average Seabee age was thirty-seven at the time the unit was founded. These were men with lots of experience, who had all chosen to leave their careers voluntarily to fight, and build, for their country.

And what could better represent this than a big statue of an angry bee wielding tools and a machine gun? Certainly not a beaver—but it almost did. At the Quonset Point Naval Base where the Seabees were born worked a man named Frank J. Iafrate, who would draw sketches of the officers who came to his office to study construction designs. One of those officers was assigned to the First Construction Detachment, and asked Iafrate to draw him a cartoony insignia that could represent the unit. Iafrate's first thought was the beaver, but some quick research showed that beavers turn tail and run when confronted with danger.

The Fighting Seabees. You can forget about getting any honey.

Iafrate then settled on the bee, who works diligently until you interrupt his work, at which point he stings you until you learn to leave him alone. And that's exactly like the construction battalions. As an added bonus, construction battalion is abbreviated as CB, pronounced *sea bee*. Get it?

Thus, the Seabee was born, and on March 5, 1942, the construction battalion was officially given the name Seabees, and the bee insignia was approved. The only change to Iafrate's original design was the removal of a *Q* that stood for Quonset Point—the navy wanted the logo to represent the Seabees from all over the country, not just Rhode Island. But Rhode Island is where they were born. And thus Iafrate built the Seabee statue that stands in front of the Seabee Museum, at the site of the former U.S. Naval Construction Battalion Center.

You may even meet former Seabees if you visit the statue. I randomly ran into Donald Gover, who was part of the 146th Battallion that landed on Normandy, where they did everything from making runways to destroying mines in the ocean. He later spent two years in Okinawa, preparing for Japan's invasion. He used model TD18 bulldozers to build during WWII, and was visiting Quonset Point to find one, but shared with me the Seabee motto, "The difficult we do immediately, the impossible takes a little longer." There are apparently numerous Seabee mottos, including the original "Construimus, Batuimus" (Latin for "We build, we fight"), and the pithy "Can Do," in reference to the Seabee ability to build large structures while under attack.

In spite of Seabees going everywhere from Iwo Jima to Iraq, most people still wouldn't have heard of them if not for John Wayne's movie *The Fighting Seabees* in 1944. The movie created some buzz about the Seabees, which is good, because it took the sting out of being mostly underappreciated before then. Meanwhile, if you want to see a giant bee with a machine gun and various construction tools (and why wouldn't you?), then just drive on down to the Seabee Museum (401–294–7233) at 21 Iafrate Way in Davisville, North Kingstown.

241

THE TALE OF UNFORTUNATE HANNAH

Chances are, you're familiar with various tales of star-crossed lovers, forced to hide from their families who hate their suitors, and meeting only in secret before running off together to live happily ever after. And you may think that stories like Romeo and Juliet's are the invention of writers like William Shakespeare. But a very similar love story actually took place centuries ago, in Rhode Island.

Rowland Robinson was the son of governor William Robinson, and held a mansion east of Pettaquamscutt Rock. Rowland was a prosperous farmer, planter, and slaveholder, and lived in the mansion with his daughter, Hannah. Hannah was renowned throughout the state for her beauty, which was the subject of much discussion and agreed upon by almost everyone. While the world seemed to be interested in Hannah Robinson, she had eyes for one person—a Mr. Peter Simons, whom she had met while attending school in Newport. Mr. Simons was a teacher at the school, and like everyone else, was entranced by Hannah's beauty.

Unfortunately, Rowland Robinson was strongly against their relationship. Though Hannah may have sang, "Please, Mr. Robinson, Peter loves me more than you can know, whoa, whoa, whoa," it did little to convince her father. He became angry and took extreme measures to keep her away from Mr. Simons, including assigning servants to act as her constant escort. He was constantly suspicious of her comings and goings, and would follow her on every trip, often demanding that she return home at once and accusing her of conspiring to meet up with her swain. To be fair, his suspicions were not unfounded: Simons would occasionally talk to her while hiding in a lilac bush beneath her window, but Robinson eventually found Simons's hiding spot, and the teacher narrowly escaped with his life.

Hannah and Simons eventually decided to elope. During a visit to her aunt's house, she escaped the care of the servant who was escorting her, and rode off in a carriage with Simons to Providence, where they were married. Rowland Robinson, unsurprisingly, was furious. He offered a bounty not only for the return of his daughter, but also on the heads of those who had assisted in her elopement. In the meantime, he disinherited his daughter in retribution for her unapproved union.

While Hannah believed that true love did not need wealth, reality proved otherwise. Once she had no money, Simons began to neglect her and would disappear for weeks at a time. Hannah grew ill, but her father refused to talk with her. Robinson eventually went to Providence to visit her, but refused to enter the house until she would renounce her marriage. A short time later, when he was sent word that Hannah was in mortal danger from her illness, Robinson finally softened his heart enough to forgive his daughter and ordered her brought home. She was carried home, but then died.

True love does not always end happily. Such is the tale of Unfortunate Hannah.

Job of the Hut

North Kingstown

If you've traveled around the country a lot, it's possible that you've seen some long buildings that look like half a cylinder, and wondered what the heck they were. What they are now can be anything from a movie house to a farmer's storage to an airplane hangar, but what they all used to be were U.S. Navy buildings. These bizarre little structures are called Quonset huts, and they were invented at Quonset Point in North Kingstown back in 1941, which is how they got the name.

Back in World War II, the navy realized that they would need a cheap, lightweight, and portable shelter that was easy to transport and assemble. So their Bureau of Yards and Docks turned to the George A. Fuller construction company in New York, with a request for an incredibly quick turnaround time: The shelters had to be designed and readied for production and manufactured all within a month. Necessity is the mother of invention, and the engineers were swift to get some plans together. The Quonset hut is thought by many to be a Native American

The Quonset hut may not be pretty, but it helped us win the war.

invention, which isn't quite true, at least not directly. The name sounds Native American, because Quonset is an Algonquian word, and the huts themselves bear a more-than-passing resemblance to Iroquois longhouses that were used as council lodges. Then again, they also look like giant metal Twinkies.

However, the main basis for the Quonset hut was the British Nissen hut from the First World War. The key difference between the Nissen hut and the Quonset hut is the arched design of the Quonset, which offers not only less wasted space, but a lot more structural integrity. These monsters of corrugated sheet metal were commonly 20 feet wide and 48 feet long, weighing six tons. And the important thing is that an eight-man crew could assemble one from parts the same day it arrived. This allowed the soldiers to build operational bases much faster than was previously possible, which was essential for fighting World War II. I mean, if it wasn't essential, they wouldn't have built more than 150,000 of them. Seriously. There were a few 40-by-100-foot giant Quonset huts used as warehouses, but the bulk of the Quonset huts produced were of the 20-by-48-foot variety.

The Quonset hut was redesigned slightly a few times over the course of the war, but its look is unmistakable. And you may still see them scattered across the country, even the world. Some of them were never taken down from where they were assembled, now standing guard over battlefields from a war long past. But most of the Quonset huts were sold to the public as surplus for $1,000 apiece. During a time when housing was at a premium, a 20-by-48-foot shelter for a thousand bucks seemed like a pretty good deal. Many universities used Quonset huts to help with their housing shortages as well. Naturally, farmers found them useful, and pretty soon Quonset huts were in use everywhere across America. Not bad for a giant metal Twinkie.

These days, nobody's quite sure what to do with them. Very few Quonset huts are listed on the National Register of Historic Places, since the register tends to list only buildings that remain at their original location, and Quonset huts were designed specifically to leave their original location. Quonset huts are routinely destroyed to make room for new development, such as recently in Kentucky and Colorado, but one place that accords Quonset huts their proper respect is their birthplace in Rhode Island.

Sure, some people call them eyesores. But the Seabees know that building Quonset huts is what helped America win the war. And so in Davisville (also known as Quonset), North Kingstown, Quonset huts are being restored near the Seabee Museum. While other states may throw away their giant metal Twinkies, Rhode Island knows that the Quonset huts held the real-estate secret to winning the war: relocation, relocation, relocation.

Putting the Moon in Moonstone

South Kingstown

Moonstone Beach in South Kingstown was so named because it was covered in moonstones—not actually rocks from the moon, but pieces of silicate that had been smoothed and polished by the ocean. In spite of these pretty shiny rocks, Moonstone Beach is more famous for the wildlife you can see there. Bird enthusiasts have frequented the beach for many years, but in the past few decades, the view has changed somewhat. The beach is now a habitat for plover. (It used to be . . . a nude beach. Decades ago, nude beaches were more common, but Moonstone Beach was one of the last holdouts in the New England area.) A local chapter of the Audubon Society (a group devoted to protecting ecosystems for birds, named for noted bird painter John James Audubon) had owned the land as a wildlife sanctuary for some time, but had leased it to the town of South Kingston to use as a public beach, of which a portion was traditionally nude. Resultantly, many of the beautiful moonstones on the beach surface would lie largely disregarded, as people were looking elsewhere.

In 1980 the Audubon Society ran out of money and transferred the property into the hands of the U.S. Fish & Wildlife Service (USFWS). The government tried to crack down on the nude sunbathing that was happening on Moonstone Beach, but a bunch of the nudists went to federal court in 1981 and argued that no laws existed that prohibited nudity just because the land was federally owned. But this all ended up being a moot point: In the mid-1980s the USFWS added the piping plover to the federal Endangered Species List. They closed much of Moonstone Beach to provide a refuge for the birds, and by 1987 all of the beach that was formerly nude was now clothed in fences.

> Once a beach with a naturalist flair,
> Moonstone's no longer nude, so beware.
> The pro-wildlife herds
> Made the beach safe for birds,
> But they don't very much care for bare.

Environmentalists view the beach as a success story, because plover require a relatively unspoiled habitat to live in, and the beach had been down to only four of them by some accounts. Less than two decades later, the population has grown to well over a hundred plover, thanks to large fenced-off areas of beach. The chicks are very vulnerable in their infancy, in fact, the entire beach is closed from April to mid-September to continue helping the birds.

For the nudists, Moonstone Beach is a sadder story. Not only was their nude beach taken away, but the USFWS got the Rhode Island state courts to change their laws to redefine nudity as disorderly conduct. To this day, tourists reading outdated guides show up at Moonstone

Beach, go for a little nude sunbathe or hike, and end up in jail with $125 bail. So if you like the piping plover, or want to see a beautiful beach with shiny stones, head on down to Moonstone. But if you "forget" to bring your clothes, don't say you weren't warned.

Back to the Grind
South Kingstown

If you visit the Kenyon Grist Mill in Usquepaugh, South Kingstown, you'll see that they are now grinding cornmeal in the new mill building that was built to replace the old one. But this shouldn't disappoint any history buffs too much, because the "new" building was built in 1886. The old mill was built way back in 1711, but floods from the Queens River destroyed it. Learning that the three most important words when building a grist mill are *location, location, location,* Bishop Philander Chase built the first mill on the current site back in 1826.

According to legend, the bishop was digging the millrace (the spot for the mill wheel) across a neck in the river, and the process was taking forever. Bishop Chase then called upon his powers as a member of the Protestant Episcopal Church and prayed to God for a little help, and lo and behold, rains came for days on end and caused a flood to cover the entire area. When the floodwaters receded, it was discovered that the added volume in the river had eroded the land right where the bishop had been digging, and had done most of his work for him. Miracles of this magnitude brought the bishop great respect, in spite of the fact that his name was Philander Chase. Honestly, what kind of name is that for a bishop?

Regardless of his unfortunate appellation, Bishop Chase finished his mill and used it as a sawmill, providing lumber for Kenyon College. Once he'd finished lumbering towards that goal, he built a gristmill in its place. That mill was eventually destroyed and replaced in 1846, and changed hands a few times before landing in those of James Dial in 1881. He installed some new turbines and replaced all the milling equipment, essentially creating the mill building that is still used today. But even after that, it wasn't all smooth sailing.

More floods came, and these weren't sent by Bishop Philander Chase. A 1908 flood destroyed the bridges leading to the mill, leaving farmers no way to bring their grain unless they felt like fording a river. And a 1913 flood diverted the water into a new channel away from the one Bishop Chase had dug, leaving the mill temporarily without power.

Runs of luck like that are what caused the mill to close at the end of 1948. But Paul Drumm Jr. and Paul

Just a picture of the Kenyon Mill. How corny.

Drumm III took over the mill in 1971, and reopened it. They even kept the same gigantic granite millstones, quarried for the mill long ago from nearby Westerly, famous for having particularly hardy granite. And sure enough, the granite has lasted—the two-and-a-half-ton runner stone still grinds cornmeal and flour the way it used to. Stone-ground meal and flour is less common today than it used to be, with most large factories steel-grinding their flour, but the Kenyon Grist Mill is more traditional. In fact, the Kenyon staff learned their craft from a Narragansett Indian named Charlie Walmsley, so they're well familiar with stone-ground milling traditions.

This is why Paul Drumm knows how to keep his nose to the grindstone—literally. Smelling for granite dust to make sure the stones aren't too close together is just one of the many secrets of milling. The others involve things like agitating a "shoe" by spinning a "damsel" and dropping grain to a "boot" and then an "eye," where it is pushed by "sweepers."

What the heck does all of that mean? It means that Kenyon Grist Mill grinds tasty flint cornmeal with the white corn essential for making johnnycakes—a Rhode Island tradition. If you want to see for yourself, the mill is open to the public on weekends from noon to 5:00 P.M. For more information call 1–800–7KENYON or visit www.kenyongristmill.com.

GO, JOHNNYCAKES, GO, GO, GO

Naturally, the best thing you can do with flint-ground white cornmeal is to make johnnycakes, or jonnycakes. Which way you spell it doesn't really matter. Heck, you can call them ashcakes, battercakes, corncakes, hoecakes, or even something more creative.

These cornmeal flatbread pancake delicacies date back to when Native Americans taught the Pilgrims how to harvest corn and cook with it. Some people call the cake "jonakin," after an old Indian term. Others call it "Shawnee cake," because it was first showed to the Pilgrims by the Shawnee Indians. And still others call it "journey cake," because the flat-baked cornmeal was ideal food for travelers (and looks oddly similar to the Lembas from *Lord of the Rings* . . .).

Regardless of what you call it, most Rhode Islanders call them delicious. The recipe is so ingrained in the Rhode Island cultural consciousness that at one time there was an official recipe for johnnycakes that began with the following instruction: "First, take an appropriate amount of mix." However, as the cakes are not as familiar to the new generation, a slightly more detailed recipe is provided below. Long ago all you needed was stone-ground white cornmeal, salt water, and a hot rock. The modern recipe adds a touch of sugar (optional), and replaces the hot rock with a hot buttered pan (recommended).

Take one cup of white flint-ground cornmeal, ideally from Kenyon Grist Mill. Mix in a teaspoon of salt and/or a teaspoon of sugar. Add one and one-third cups of boiling water until you have a stiff dough. Drop the dough onto a hot buttered pan as if you were making pancakes, keeping in mind that johnnycakes need to cook much longer, and voilà! You are a Native American chef.

Horsing Around (and Around, and Around)
Westerly

If a girl tells you that she'll go out with you when pigs fly, she probably means never. But if a girl tells you that she'll go out with you when horses fly, clearly you should take her on a date to the Flying Horse Carousel at Watch Hill in Westerly. This merry-go-round features a score of horses that really fly: Instead of being attached by poles to a rotating floor, they are suspended by large chains from above. The hand-carved wooden horses fly over the dirt ground below, swinging out to fly farther away from the center as the ride speeds up. There are even metal rings for the kids to grab as they pass, and the last one is the proverbial brass ring, granting the grabber a free ride. It's a whole lot of fun.

Only the chains keep these horses from taking flight.

So much fun, in fact, that it could well be hazardous to adults, who aren't used to such frenzied heights of enjoyment. For this reason, the carousel only allows children to ride. Well, okay, the other reason is because the horses are suspended from above and a little smaller than those found on most carousels, but most carousels consist of plastic seats on a rotating floor, pretending to be horses.

The Flying Horse Carousel is not only the last running carousel with actual flying horses, but is considered by many to be the oldest carousel in the country. It was manufactured by the Charles W. Dare Company sometime between 1867 and 1876, with incredible crafts-manship. Each horse is hand-carved from a single piece of wood, and is embellished with a real horsehair mane and tail, glass agate eyes, and leather saddle. And flying, did we mention the flying?

The carousel was originally part of a traveling carnival, a giant merry-go-round toted around from place to place by a horse. In the early 1880s the carnival could not move the merry-go-round anymore, and thus it was left at Watch Hill, where it was permanently installed. If you believe the local legends, the horse that once dragged the carousel around was so connected to it that upon his death, his tail was cured and became one of the twenty real horsehair tails on the carousel that remain today. Which horse is it? We're not telling. But if you know any kids who like flying horses, maybe they can go for a ride and find out.

The Flying Horse Carousel (401–348–6007) is located on Bay Street and is open June 15 through Labor Day, from 1:00 to 9:00 P.M. Tickets are only a buck for the kids, but sadly, no amount of money can buy you a ride if you're over twelve years old.

Tarzan Brown
Westerly

The most famous runner ever to come out of Rhode Island was as famous for his exploits off the track as on. Westerly's Ellison Brown was a natural athlete from a young age, where as part of the Narragansett Indian tribe his name was Deerfoot. But he was known to the rest of the world as Tarzan Brown, a nickname he was given for his propensity to climb trees and swing from the branches.

Tarzan Brown was not the first famous Narragansett runner. Before him there was Horatio "Chief" Stanton, already well-known by the time Brown was born. One day Stanton was running 14 miles from Westerly to Shannock to watch a baseball game. Upon arriving, he exclaimed to his coach, "Some kid has been following me all the way from Westerly!" The coach, Tippy Salimeno, eagerly went to meet the boy, who was none other than Tarzan Brown, and told him to come back when he was sixteen, old enough to race professionally. Four years later, he did.

Brown ran his first Boston Marathon in 1933 at the age of nineteen, finishing an unimpressive thirty-second. But a year later he was struggling for first, neck and neck with favorite Clarence DeMar. DeMar ended up winning the 1934 marathon by only thirty seconds, with his claiming it was even closer than that. Brown twice passed DeMar during the race, only to fall behind again, and was neck and neck the whole last mile.

Perhaps Tarzan Brown's most famous race was in 1935. His mother had died just four days before the Boston Marathon, on April 15. His shoes were old tattered sneakers that barely held together. Shoes then were all very heavy, and not well designed for running. Running shoes weren't even manufactured in New England until 1933, when Sam Ritchings created STAR shoes. Ritchings sent a pair to DeMar just before his run in the 1934 marathon. DeMar loved the shoes, and claimed that if Brown had them, he would have beaten him that year. But Brown didn't have them, even in 1935. And his lack of good shoes had a consequence: He had to go without shoes altogether during a large chunk of the 1935 Boston Marathon.

Some say that Brown's old shoes just fell apart at mile 21. Some say his feet overheated at mile 19, so he chose to take them off. Either way, historians agree that for at least the last few miles of the marathon, Tarzan Brown ran barefoot. In spite of this, he managed to finish thirteenth. This spawned numerous legends that Brown ran complete marathons barefoot, and won. Heck, his name was Tarzan, and he did like to run through the woods barefoot. But he eventually got better shoes for competitive running.

Brown won his first marathon in 1936, when John Kelley, who was favored to win, patted him on the butt while passing him between the 20th and 21st mile, as if to say "nice try." But this seemed to energize Brown, who ran past Kelley to win. To this day, that part of the Boston Marathon is called "Heartbreak Hill," where the favorite Kelley had his heart broken. Tarzan Brown won, wearing shoes made for running.

After winning again in 1939, his participation in the Boston Marathon lessened after 1940, but he returned in 1946 to take twelfth in his final Boston Marathon appearance. However, Brown could still run. He was often challenged by locals, and always won. This, combined with his propensity to literally take bites out of his whiskey glass and chew it, made him a living legend long after he was done marathoning.

His death, sudden and unexpected, came when he was run over by a van driven by a Phillip Edwards on August 23, 1975. Reports vary as to whether Brown was a bystander killed by a random man backing over him, or whether he and Edwards had argued. Regardless, his legacy was greater recognition of the Narragansett tribe, and stories about Tarzan Brown still circulate through Rhode Island to this day.

Lucky Ducky

Westerly

As Ernie once said, a rubber ducky makes bath time so much fun. But Ernie probably couldn't conceive of how much fun is had each year on the Pawcatuck River during Westerly's annual Pawcatuck River Duck Race. The Pawcatuck River is much bigger than a bathtub, and every April a prodigious plethora of plastic manufactured mallards are dumped into it to race for charity. How plentiful a plethora? Well, in 2006, a giant bulldozer atop the Pawcatuck Bridge dumped 20,000 ducks into the river, each one purchased for $5.00.

So what does $5.00 buy? Well, first of all, it supports good causes. More than half of the money raised goes to local schools and nonprofit organizations, with the rest distributed to various Greater Westerly-Pawcatuck Chamber of Commerce programs. Fittingly, one of the big projects the race helps fund is their Duck Boat project, a plan to have an amphibious tour vessel. If it works, maybe it would be like seeing a big momma duck with all her little ducklings—though most ducks don't have 20,000 kids.

Most importantly, though, $5.00 buys you a duck and the excitement of watching it float down the river neck and neck, er, bill and bill with 19,999 other rubber duckies. It is a gloriously bizarre sight to see 20,000 rubber ducks floating down a river. And if your duck is one of the first hundred to finish, you win a prize, which could be anything from a gift certificate to the grand prize of a trip to Disney World.

But even if your duck is shipped away in the losers' boat, the crowd of ducks in the river combined with the crowd of people wearing duck paraphernalia make this event everything it's quacked up to be. For more information call 1–800–732–7636 or e-mail info@westerly chamber.org.

WASHINGTON COUNTY

Pulling Strings
Westerly

"Say kids, what time is it?" If you don't know that the answer is "It's Howdy Doody time!" then you probably weren't around in the 1940s and '50s. The *Howdy Doody Show* on NBC was one of the most popular shows on television at the time, starring Buffalo Bob Smith and his freckle-faced marionette, Howdy Doody. But here's something that even most Howdy Doody fans don't know: For a number of years, Howdy Doody lived in a very small bank vault in Westerly.

How did one of the world's most beloved puppets end up in a safe-deposit box in Rhode Island? I'm glad you asked. In 1967, seven years after the *Howdy Doody Show* went off the air, the show's puppeteer, Rufus Rose, wrote a letter to NBC promising to donate the original Howdy Doody puppet to the Detroit Institute of Arts upon his death. Eight years later, in 1975, Rufus Rose passed away. And that's where the trouble began. Before he died, Rose had lent the puppet to Buffalo Bob from the show, who needed it to earn money. Buffalo Bob toured with Howdy Doody for years and finally returned it to the Rose family in 1998, when they agreed to sell the puppet and split the profit with him. But Buffalo Bob then died.

The Rose family still wanted to sell the puppet, but the Detroit Institute of Arts claimed that Rufus Rose wanted it to go to the museum, and NBC said that they only gave him the puppet in the first place with that understanding. The Rose family, meanwhile, claimed that Rufus's letter was never a legal contract. The disputed puppet was valued at $50,000, and since the parties could not reach an agreement, it ended up in a safe-deposit box in Westerly. Howdy Doody stayed locked in a vault in Rhode Island while his case was heard in court.

But the Rose family argued that it wasn't the original puppet. In addition to the original Howdy Doody, there were many copies, because puppets can break but the show must go on. Double Doody was a backup puppet that now rests in the Smithsonian. Photo Doody was used for publicity photos. Even Original Doody wasn't the original, because the actual original Howdy Doody disappeared as soon as the show fired its creator. Nonetheless, the judge was no dummy, and found against the Rose family. In 2001 Howdy Doody was shipped out of state to the Detroit Institute of Arts—but we hear he still misses Rhode Island.

Twelfth Night
Westerly

When Christmas and New Year's are over, most people start winding down. But things are just getting started for the Chorus of Westerly, who have been presenting "A Celebration of Twelfth Night" every year since 1975. The celebration is an expansively produced event, a combination holiday pageant, medieval feast, play, dance, and musical, featuring, of course, lots of singing (after all, it is put on by a chorus). The 2007 performance included nearly 100 actors and 200 chorus members. Characters range from jesters to sheep, with cast members as young as four years old. There are songs sung from various centuries and countries as the story moves through the ages, jumping from things like forest spirits to Baba Yaga to Father Christmas.

As if that weren't enough, the celebration is punctuated by the Peasants' Feast, which is a medieval banquet served by costumed actors. Dining on roast pork is certainly no boar, especially with traditional entertainment during the meal that has in the past included fiddles, bagpipes, Morris dancing, and a brass orchestra. You'll want to order tickets well before the early January performance date by contacting the Chorus of Westerly at (401) 596–8663 or visiting their Web site at www.chorusofwesterly.org.

And yes, as a renowned chorus that has been around for nearly fifty years, they have other performances throughout the year as well. But if you're only going to catch one night, you should make it the twelfth one.

You'd have to be really pig-headed to skip this celebration.

Fawkes You, Beach
Westerly

Long ago in England, a man named Guy Fawkes tried to blow up Parliament. It didn't work, and the English have been celebrating Guy Fawkes Day ever since. But lately another group of people have been celebrating Guy Fawkes Day: the Misquamicut Players. For the past ten years they've been putting on a show to reenact Fawkes's execution in early October, complete with a bonfire.

There's acting, music, dancing, and burning—all the elements needed for a good party. Due largely to the bonfire (or due to the large bonfire—take your pick), the party is held on Misquamicut Beach in Westerly. And most importantly, it's entirely free. So really, there's no reason not to come hear bagpipes, taste cider, touch the sand, smell the bonfire, and see Guy Fawkes executed. Well, the one reason might be rain: They usually postpone the event for a day if it's pouring. Otherwise, though, you should plot to check it out.

The annual Guy Fawkes Bonfire Night takes place at the Andrea Hotel, 89 Atlantic Avenue. For more information visit www.misquamicut.org.

Nothing brings people together like a good execution.

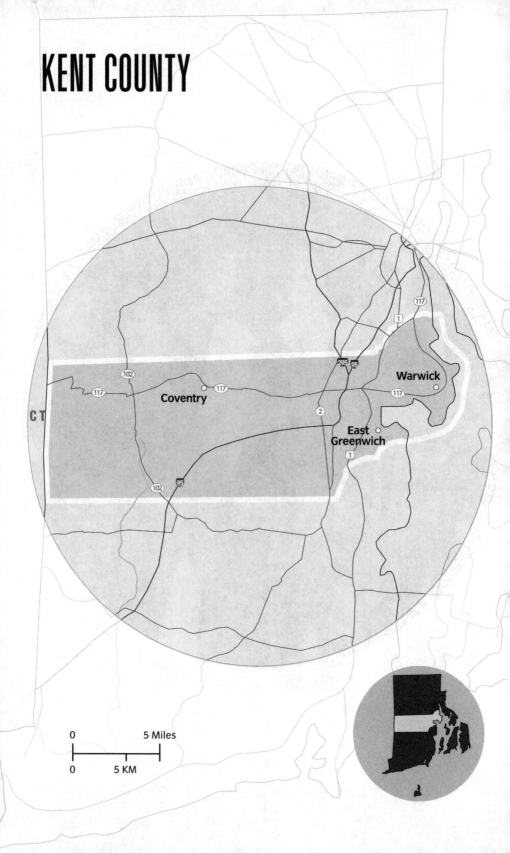

KENT COUNTY

Coventry

Warwick

East
Greenwich

C T

0   5 Miles

0   5 KM

KENT COUNTY

The Great Pumpkin
Coventry

Even Charlie Brown would have to be impressed by the pumpkin that won the Southern New England Giant Pumpkin Growers (SNEGPG) Championship in 2006. The pumpkin, weighing in at 1,502 pounds, set a new world record. And oddly enough, the world's largest pumpkin was grown in the smallest state: Rhode Island. What isn't at all odd is the fact that the man who grew it was Ron Wallace, of Coventry.

Ron Wallace knows a lot about giant pumpkins. He has to, because Ron is president of the Southern New England Giant Pumpkin Growers Association (and yes, also a client). And you don't just go about growing the world's largest pumpkin on dumb luck. He has been researching and growing giant pumpkins for many years. His pumpkin from 2000 was giant by normal standards, but at 881 pounds, not nearly as large as his 2006 effort. However, Ron was serious about growing giant pumpkins. He continued studying up. He attended various seminars and conferences about pumpkins. He even moved, just to be in an area where his pumpkins could get better soil and sunlight. Twice. And in 2006, Ron estimates that he spent thirty hours a week just tending to his plants.

"Pumpkin growing is a lot of work," says Ron, "and you just have to stick with it." Well, all of this work paid off. His pumpkin ended up growing roughly 35 pounds a day, and when it came time for the 2006 SNEGPG Championship, Ron squashed the competition with his 1,502-pound behemoth. The victory earned him a place in the *Guinness Book of World Records,* an appearance on *The Martha Stewart Show,* and an invitation as the guest of honor at the 2007 International Giant Vegetable Growers Convention, where he received an orange jacket. But the sweetest thing of all is victory that comes from hard work—although a close second is a prodigious amount of pumpkin pies.

The world's biggest pumpkin. Other competitors are Greene with envy.

Steam Room

East Greenwich

Rhode Island has a history of great inventors and industry, but today it seems as if most people are forgetting this history—and that has Bob Merriam steamed up. That's why he started the New England Wireless and Steam Museum, to preserve and honor the engineering achievements from a century ago.

Bob comes from a family that knows about New England's industrial past. Like his father before him, Bob went to Harvard's engineering school and worked as an engineer. He taught engineering at Swarthmore, and his grandparents and relatives all love industrial history. Bob felt Rhode Island's industrial history was being ignored, so with the help of some like-minded friends and a little *engine-uity,* he started a small museum in an old cow barn.

Thomas Edison used this type of engine. Bright idea.

Now more than forty years later, the East Greenwich museum has five buildings, including a classic New England meeting hall and the world's oldest surviving radio station. Walter Massie of Providence built this wireless radio station for Point Judith back in 1907. In 1912 a judge declared that Guglielmo Marconi (who, coincidentally, was born the same year as Massie) had the patent, so Massie's station was declared illegal. It was later slated to be torn down, but the owner donated the building, and Massie's son donated his father's equipment. Thus the wireless radio station now survives, and is on the National Register of Historic Places.

Of course, there are plenty of steam engines as well. The collection includes engines made by Armington & Sims, a Providence manufacturer that made the engines used by Thomas Edison. Or you can see Hartford, Connecticut's original generator from 1883, which still works so well that Bob can disconnect the museum from the national power grid and light the whole building with their own engines.

The whole operation is run by volunteers, so don't drop by without calling to schedule an appointment first: (401) 885–0545. If you really love steam engines, you'll want to attend their annual Great Yankee Steam-Up. Details can be found at http://users.ids.net/~newsm.

Send in the Clowns
East Greenwich

Some people are terrified of clowns, but they probably never got to hang out at Clown Town when they were young. What is Clown Town? Well, it's an annual fund-raiser put on by the Greenwich Bay Women's Club where many people dress up as . . . you guessed it, clowns. The clowns run various games for young children, ranging from fish-catching to beanbag-tossing. And since young children generally don't like losing at games, everyone who plays a game wins. So even if your four-year-old can't toss a beanbag through a hole, he'll still get a prize. In addition to the plethora of games, there is also a copious amount of food, because every fund-raiser needs to include a bake sale. Between the food, the games, and the people dressed as clowns, the kids tend to stay pretty entertained.

Who says clowning around never helped anyone?

The organizers stay entertained, too, because all the money raised is put back into the community. Clown Town has been successful since its inception, having now run for more than forty years. Some people who remember going as children have grown up to bring their own children. I even remember attending once or twice in my own youth, eager to play lots of games and stuff myself with cookies by running around in Swift Gym in East Greenwich, where it is held each spring. Now that I'm grown up, though, I play games and stuff myself with cookies at home. But my house has fewer clowns, so if you have any young children, you should bring them to Clown Town instead.

To find out when Clown Town will occur this year, check out the Greenwich Bay Women's Club Web site at www.gbwc.org.

A Jigger of Syrup
East Greenwich

Jigger's Diner in East Greenwich is one of the original dining cars built by the famed Worcester Dining Car Company, but its history goes back far further than that: It goes back to a man whose nickname was Jigger. What kind of man takes the nickname Jigger? A man whose real name is Vilgot Lindberg. After all, would you go to a diner called Vilgot's?

Lindberg didn't think so either, which is why he started his diner business as Lindy's back in 1917. He sold hotdogs and hamburgers in a building next door to the current Jigger's location. Why next door? Because the Borden Brothers had a lunch cart there until 1928, when it moved to Wickford and Lindberg opened a new upscale diner on that spot. How upscale? Full dinners were served by men in dress shirts and ties. And it must have been pretty good food, too, because legend has it that behind every person eating at a stool stood three more eagerly awaiting their turn.

In 1941 Lindberg left the restaurant business to sell hardware. Lenny Boren was the next owner, who decided to replace the old diner with a bigger one in June 1950. That bigger diner was ordered from the Worcester Dining Car Company and brought in on a flatbed truck. Between 1950 and 1983 the diner changed owners faster than it changed menus. A partial list of owners includes Fred Freedlund, Bob "Frenchy" Filteau, Bert Johnson, Ernie Cataline, Norman Harris, and Clarence "Ike" Huling. In 1983 it looked like Jigger's Diner had given up the ghost, and it closed its doors.

One of the original diners.

But then Carol Shriner began restoring the diner in January 1992. And the restoration was a big job: The only things remaining from the original dining car aside from the woodwork and tiles were the clock and a few green stools. She brought in booths and a pastry case from another diner in Massachusetts, and got some red stools from Iowa. The stainless-steel hood was refurbished in accordance with old photos of the original diner, and by the summer of 1992, Jigger's was open for business once more. Fifteen years later, Jigger's Diner is still going strong, complete with its shiny restored roof.

What's the secret? Well, Jigger's may look like a diner, but the food is far from standard diner fare. House specials include the Vermonticristo (ham and cheddar on raisin French toast) and gingerbread pancakes. And on Fridays Jigger's becomes even less dinerlike and offers a gourmet BYOB dinner, complete with candles and wine glasses. Dishes on the Friday dinner menu rotate, and have included London broil with garlic-Parmesan mashed potatoes, grilled shrimp and vegetables over linguine, and chicken breast wrapped with pancetta on tomato-basil pappardelle. And in case fancy fare doesn't please the little ones, Jigger's also caters to kids by offering grilled cheese sandwiches and hot dogs. Current owner Iva Reyhout likes the kids. In fact, Reynhout says, "I love the people, I love to cook, I love to work with everybody."

And she'd love to have you come by for a meal. You will find Jigger's Diner (401–884–5388) at 145 Main Street.

Spray It, Don't Say It

East Greenwich

East Greenwich gets hit with graffiti every summer. But unlike most towns hit with graffiti, they're glad, because it's part of their annual Great Graffiti Contest. For five years now the town of East Greenwich and their housing authority have held a contest that actually promotes graffiti. Of course, they don't promote it happening all over the town, only on the street they set aside for the event. Still, it's nice to see street painters who are usually scorned by authorities finally get a chance to show off their skills, and maybe even win prizes.

Yes, prizes. There is a cash prize for the best art by anyone over the age of seventeen, and because it's a family-friendly event, there is a prize for the best graffiti by an eleven-to-sixteen-year-old. And then,

Graffiti should be appreciated more often.

because family-friendly events love kids, there is a prize for the best graffiti by a kid ten years or younger. Why would you ever give spray paint to a kid that young? Well, maybe you wouldn't, which is why the event also provides colored chalk for would-be artists under ten years of age. After the painting ends, a block party begins with free drinks and snacks. So even if you aren't artistically talented, you can pop down to London Street. After all, when else can you drink, celebrate graffiti, and have the police approve?

Dinner and a Movie
East Greenwich

The Touro Fraternal Association consists of hundreds of Jewish men from all over Rhode Island. And every year on Christmas, they rent out a restaurant for exclusive use by their members.

Dinner and a Movie Night started many years ago on Christmas, when two members saw each other at the China Buffet in East Greenwich and realized they'd seen each other at the same restaurant the previous year. Two hours later they saw each other at the same movie theater that they'd seen each other at the previous year. It was at this point that they decided to begin sponsoring Dinner and a Movie Night every Christmas for their fraternal organization. They rented out an entire Chinese buffet and invited members to sign up to eat and then get tickets to any show at the movie theater across the

When it's Christmas, what's fun for a Jew?
Chinese food and a movie to view.
Touro knows this is so;
Each year's party they throw
Bring in quite a few who view and chew.

street. It was a grand success. In recent years Dinner and a Movie Night has became so popular that not only do they need to rent out the whole restaurant, but they have to do an early seating and a late seating.

For more information check out their Web site at www.tourofraternal .org.

Avoiding Odium
East Greenwich

The Greenwich Odeum is a small theater in a small town in a small state. Given all that, many are surprised by some of the big names that perform there, from the Count Basie Orchestra to Roomful of Blues. Performers like these probably do it for two reasons. First of all, they appreciate the atmosphere. The building was originally built as a vaudeville house back in the 1920s, and although it was eventually converted to a movie theater, today's entertainers can perhaps feel the history as they perform on stage.

The audience certainly appreciates the atmosphere, especially the luxurious amount of leg room afforded by the super-wide rows. When the Odeum reopened the former theater in 1994, they removed nearly half the seats, resulting in an unrivaled experience where you don't trip over anyone getting to your seat, and can stretch out during the show without kicking the people in front of you. And even more importantly, the people behind you can do the same.

The other main reason to like the Odeum is that the whole theater is run by volunteers. Volunteers are the ones who transformed a closed movie theater into a working performance theater, and volunteers continue to run the entire nonprofit operation. Not only are they nonprofit, but they host fund-raisers for various charitable organizations. In spite of what the name might sound like, there is no odium at the Odeum.

What there is at the Odeum is a varied performance schedule, including theater like Shakespeare and music like folk legend Tommy Makem. I've seen his show a few years running, and he always says it's one of his favorite places to perform. Chances are, he's never said that about anywhere else. Anyway, to check what's playing at the Odeum, you can call (401) 885–9119, visit www.greenwichodeum.org, or just drop by—it's right in the middle of Main Street. And, seriously, about the spacious seating: Your legs will thank you.

Irish folk music and an incredible amount of leg room: A winning combination.

Culinary Stamp of Approval

East Greenwich

If you go to the Post Office Cafe at 11 Main Street in East Greenwich, you won't have to settle for licking envelopes. The former post office was reopened by Steve Marra and Bill Pinelli as a moderately upscale Italian restaurant in 1994, with plenty of pasta and various other tasty dishes.

Looking for a place to eat? Go ahead, go postal.

While "post office" may not seem as attractive a dining theme as "hard rock" or "Australian outback," the atmosphere is very pleasant. The food is good enough that you don't mind looking around and thinking, "I can't believe I'm eating in an oddly redecorated post office."

By contrast, attempting to eat a picnic on the floor of the current East Greenwich Post Office is highly unsatisfying. If given the option, I highly recommend the Post Office Cafe (401–885–4444) instead.

The April Fools
East Greenwich

April Fools' Day is one of those holidays that never seem to get official recognition. But in Rhode Island, they know how to celebrate it. In fact, they have an annual Rhode Island Comedy Festival each year over the weekend of April Fools', celebrated by . . . well, April fools. What does this comedy festival consist of? Why, lots of comedy, of course. In years past the festival has included everything from comedic magicians for kids to comedy contests to professional stand-up to sketches lampooning local issues. And it's all masterminded by funnyman Charlie Hall.

Charlie Hall, in addition to being a nationally known stand-up comic and cartoonist, is also the creator of the Ocean State Follies, a Rhode Island performance group that parodies the state's politics and peccadilloes. In 2004 the Greenwich Odeum asked Hall to book a Follies show and wanted some stand-up comedy later that year. Hall decided that both comedic events should happen at the same time and a contest should be added as well, and thus was born the Rhode Island Comedy Festival. "It was a fairly easy delivery," says Hall, "but I still have the stretch marks."

In the weeks before the festival, there is an open stand-up comedy contest to be named the "Funniest Person in Rhode Island," with anyone with sufficient courage (and an entry fee) encouraged to do their best three to five minutes of stand-up comedy. Then the festival proper features a slew of local stand-ups the first night, capped off with the winner of the Funniest Person contest. The next night has various comedic entertainment called "The April Fools!" beginning with Charlie Hall's Ocean State Follies performing their sketches and songs mocking the state. (Charlie himself does a mean impression of a mean former governor who demanded that a closed store reopen to provide him with plastic forks.) And it finishes off with more stand-up comedy; Hall's time on the stand-up circuit has given him a fair (or perhaps unfair) number of connections.

"I've known almost all the comics and acts for years," says Hall. "I knew whom to call." And indeed, many of the comedians were friends of his who began as he did at Periwinkles Comedy Club in Providence. The 2006 festival featured two of them: local favorite Frank O'Donnell and Ed "The Machine" Regine, whose act detailed a system for giving idiots a certain number of marbles that they had to relinquish upon saying or doing stupid things. And while gathering all of his old friends together to share stories is half the fun, Hall believes that an important part of the festival is promoting comedy in the state and showcasing homegrown talent: "I love helping newcomers to break in . . . there aren't that many venues to perform anymore." And, unlike usual, he's not fooling.

For more information visit www.ricomedyfestival.com.

ANCHORS AWAY

Most children who grew up in East Greenwich the past thirty years have climbed atop the mighty anchor in the middle of Academy Field at 111 Pierce Street. But few of them know where it came from—I didn't, and I'd been sitting atop that anchor for years.

The anchor was loaned to East Greenwich by the federal government in 1977 to celebrate the 300th anniversary of the town's founding in 1677. Why just a loan? Well, the government may one day decide they want it back, so the loan is renewed every ten years. Meanwhile, it serves as a perfect symbol of the town and state. Not only is the anchor featured on the state flag, but on the East Greenwich coat of arms as well. So until the government becomes stern and ships off our anchor, it remains used for sea voyages of the imaginary kind.

When you're young, it looks like a giant metal goose. Honestly.

The Cutting Edge
Warwick

Matt The Knife (MTK to his friends) likes to perform. One of the things he performs is magic, but don't call him a magician, because he hates that. He also performs mentalistic feats, but doesn't like being called a mentalist. In fact, if you were to break the world of magic into thirteen forms plus various allied arts, you could say that Matt does everything except children's magic.

So what does he like to be called? Simple: Matt The Knife. His actual name is Matthew Cassiere, but nobody pronounces it right. He's an accomplished cardsharp, about whom people have said, "Matt's so sharp, you could use him to cut." Add this to Matt's love for jazz, and Matt The Knife is a perfect nickname. And it's catchy enough that I was humming it the whole day before I talked to him.

But Matt The Knife doesn't just cut, he breaks. Specifically, he breaks world records and has broken eleven at the time of this writing, usually multiple records a year. He currently holds the world record for fastest escape from handcuffs, fastest one-handed cutting of a deck of cards, fastest escape from a straitjacket, fastest fire-eating, longest torch-teething, and a few group records as well. As recently as the beginning of 2007, he went to China and set a new world record for fastest underwater escape from handcuffs.

Like Batman, Matt's skills come from a lifetime of studying and training to be a super-spy. Unlike Batman, he began with a more questionable moral code. "I was a grifter, con man, cardsharp . . . I ran a pickpocket ring from Boston to New York, and ran a high-end shoplifting ring," says Matt. As soon as his first job at a fast-food joint proved disappointing, he embarked on a life of crime. Skills Matt had learned in his youth out of a desire to copy James Bond suddenly became useful, because cheating at cards, picking locks, and sleight of hand can all be lucrative.

Many small blades of grass. One big blade of not grass.

Unfortunately, criminal activities can also get you (and your friends) shot, so Matt eventually decided to go straight. He began working with anti-fraud divisions, and focused his skills into a new job. Having seen stage magicians impress audiences with a small subset of his own skills, Matthew Cassiere became Matt The Knife, performer. Since then he has done countless performances of what he calls "magic with an edge," touring colleges around the country and eleven countries around the world with a show that is never the same twice. Matt claims to have literally a thousand different effects, including card tricks, sword swallowing, glass eating, glass walking, fire eating, escapes, bullet catches, Russian roulette, and many, many more. And he continues to love it. "The minute it feels like a job," explains Matt, "is the day I'll quit."

His passion shows in his work and has gained him international fame (not to mention his consulting/lecture side business, Masterful Conjurations). But conveniently, he still isn't too well-known in his own state, so he can avoid the paparazzi when he returns to Warwick. "I love traveling the world," Matt says, "but at the end of the day, I want to come home to Rhode Island."

To travel the world and realize you live where you like best, that takes a sharp man.

If you're keen, you can learn more about Matt at www.mattthe knife.com.

Ro, Ro, Ro Your Bot
Warwick

Politicians always say that children are the future. And science-fiction writers always say that robots are the future. So it makes perfect sense that the Rhode Island School of the Future (RISF) hosts a big annual event that combines children and robots. (Well, combines them in the same room; they don't go around replacing children's limbs with cybernetic enhancements, although it is very tempting.) The

Today, the kids still control the robots. Tomorrow, who knows?

annual Robotic Park event is a giant showcase where about 1,000 Rhode Island students grades K–12 show off the robotic creations they built in response to various challenges. It is the largest event of its kind in the country.

Over the school year, students are asked to design robots that imitate animal behavior, robots that interact with the audience, and Rube Goldbergian machines that start and end with the pulling of a string. Then in April, which is not coincidentally National Science and Technology Month, they all gather at the Community College of Rhode Island to show off their stuff. Robotic Park has been held since 1992, and RISF director Janice Kowalczyk is pleased with the continued success of the event. From the Lego League that has to build autonomous robots out of Legos, to the robotics parade with twenty-five floats, looking around the Robotic Park event leads the observer to one inevitable conclusion: We will be taken over by children and robots.

For more information on Robotic Park, visit www.risf.com.

The Pipes, the Pipes Are Calling
Warwick

Imagine, if you will, that one night you hear spooky noises coming from the pipes in your house. The noise is so scary and ghostlike, you aren't sure whether to call a plumber or some paranormal investigators. Luckily, you don't have to choose, because if you call Grant Wilson and Jason Hawes, you get both. Jason and Grant have been plumbers in Warwick for many years, but they also founded The Atlantic Paranormal Society (TAPS) to investigate supernatural disturbances. Haven't heard of TAPS? Well, perhaps you know them as the Ghost Hunters.

Yes, *those* Ghost Hunters, the ones with a show on the Sci-Fi Channel. They're much more famous now that they have a TV show, but despite their notoriety for investigating the paranormal, they haven't given up their plumbing jobs. While they might be flush with success, they're level-headed enough to know that TV celebrity can quickly vanish down the toilet, whereas plumbing is a job that Jason calls "recession-proof." He and Grant used to be plumbers for Roto-Rooter, and their mutual experience with supernormal events led them to form TAPS.

Other people with an interest in the paranormal soon joined, and TAPS continued to grow. Jason and Grant have acquired a lot of fancy equipment over the years, from infrared cameras to EMF meters, which they use to detect and document any evidence of paranormal activity. They tend to investigate at night because spirits that emit light or sound are easier to detect at night, because most reports of supernatural activity occur at night, and because during the day they're fixing pipes. Hey, they're still plumbers.

They now have TAPS branches across the country, and their show is watched by nearly two million people, which would be enough to put anyone in high spirits. But Jason and Grant have remained very grounded. Most of their team are blue-collar workers in the community, who all have day jobs and do this in their spare time. Jason and Grant have been best friends for many years, and even their families are close.

Their families may come first, but if you have supernatural problems, you can contact them at grant@the-atlantic-paranormal-society.com or jason@the-atlantic-paranormal-society.com. They don't even charge for investigations, though if you aren't local, they do ask that you cover the gas money. No matter what kind of spirit is haunting your house, they can deal with everything but the kitchen sink—and then they can fix the kitchen sink.

As Time Rolls On

Warwick

It used to be that anyone who lived in Warwick knew that whether for a hot date or just to have fun, Sholes Roller Rink was the best place to go for roller-skating. Let me explain for the young readers: Years ago, before the popularity of in-line skates like Roller Blades, people would entertain themselves with an activity known as "roller-skating." The people had shoes with wheels in a box shape instead of a line, and would skate around a big oval rink while trying not to fall down. It may not sound cool now, but it was cool then—*wheely* cool.

Sholes Rink was an institution, founded in 1938 by Morris Sholes and passed down through the family. Many people through the decades had romance bloom while trying to keep their balance. Even a few friends of mine had parties there when I was growing up.

Alas, in 1999 Sholes Rink closed. Like so many glorious institutions of yesteryear, it was knocked down and replaced by a hotel, a Hampton

Pieces of the original Sholes rink fresco, with replica chandelier.

UPS AND DOWNS

If you were to visit the Rocky Point Chowder House in Warwick, you'd probably have a little fun. After all, they serve three kinds of clam chowder as well as clam cakes—fried battered clam balls that are delightfully delectable. And yet, your meal would be marred by the inescapable fact that people who came here in decades gone by had much more fun than you're having now. Neener, neener, neener.

This is because Rocky Point used to be the site of a grand amusement park, which was unimaginatively called Rocky Point amusement park. When I was growing up, I'd never heard of Six Flags, but if you wanted to go to an amusement park that wasn't Disney, there was no better place than Rocky Point. Contrary to what you might expect from the name, the rides at Rocky Point were much more fun than a Pointy Rock. They had many roller coasters over the years, ranging from classic Looff coasters to bigger ones like the Cyclone and Wildcat, which some people were too scared to go on when they were growing up, not that the author of this book would know anything about that. But even terrified tykes could enjoy the flume, the Ferris wheel, the haunted house, the freefall . . . well, maybe not the freefall—it was scarier than the haunted house.

Anyway, it all began back in 1847 when Captain William Winslow bought some land on Rocky Point to use for shore dinners. Shore dinners, of course, are big seafood dinners, and the best in all of New England were at the Rocky Point Shore Dinner Hall. It was the spot to dine back in the 1920s and '30s, until 1938 when a hurricane came and destroyed both the amusement park and the dinner hall. It was rebuilt in the late 1940s only to be devastated by another hurricane in 1954. But they persevered and opened up again. And in spite of this, they still built a roller coaster called the Cyclone. Go figure.

It would be hard to say which was the bigger attraction, the amusement park with its Ferris wheel and fun houses, or the shore dinner hall with its chowder and lobster and steamed clams. The important thing was to ride the roller coaster before eating three bowls of chowder, and not the other way around. Yuck.

Alas, Rocky Point went bankrupt in 1996, and most of the rides were auctioned off. They attempted to revive it with a fair later that year, but it just wasn't the same. The park was abandoned, and after a fire in 2000, Rocky Point was sold in 2003 for $8.5 million to a developer. Word has it that there are plans to turn the former park site into a gated community, replacing family fun for everyone with . . . well, lack of fun that's largely restricted.

So if you go there today, there's no park, no roller coasters, no Ferris wheel, and no gigantic shore dinner hall that serves 1,000 people at a time with bounteous banquets including everything under the sea. All that remains is the Rocky Point Chowder House (401–739–4222), serving up chowder and clam cakes, with a heaping side order of nostalgia.

Rocky Point amusement park, now with less amusement and more rocky.

Inn to be exact. But the spirit of Sholes Rink lives on inside that hotel, especially in the lobby bar. The rink's giant frescos of celebrities and cartoons were broken into pieces and now grace the walls of the hotel bar. The bar's giant hexagonal chandeliers are metal reproductions of the paper ones from the rink. The beam ceiling, the color scheme, the cherrywood, the whole atmosphere of the hotel is made to pay homage to the once proud Sholes Rink.

Best of all, one of the current hotel employees is there as a direct result of Sholes Rink: Denise Roy now goes to work each day at the same site where her parents first met. Just goes to show, tradition keeps rolling along.

The Hampton Inn that carries on the Sholes Rink tradition is located at 2100 Post Road in Warwick. Call (401) 739–8888; the bar is open from 4:30 to midnight.

The Great Gaspee
Warwick

Most people have heard of the Boston Tea Party—big famous event, gets lots of press because some Bostonians decided to use the ocean as a giant teacup. But when it comes to really sticking it to the British, Rhode Island did it first, and Rhode Island did it better. I've always felt that Rhode Island does most things better than everyone else, but in this case, history supports me. A year before that posh little tea party, Rhode Islanders grounded a British vessel, shot the commander, and burned the ship.

In June 1772 Captain Lindsey was taking the sloop *Hannah* from Newport to Providence. At the time, the area was patrolled by a ship named the HMS *Gaspee,* commanded by a Lieutenant Dudingston, who was sent by King George to stop smuggling, which included at least half of the ships in Rhode Island at the time, so he wasn't very popular. The *Gaspee* chased Captain Lindsey, who cleverly lured the ship into some shallows near Warwick where it would run aground. With the *Gaspee* stuck on a sandbar, Lindsey went to tell the good news to John Brown, who sent Abraham Whipple with eight boats of men to capture the ship.

As stones of memoriam go, we're actually not too sad that the *Gaspee* is gone.

Boarding proved a bit tricky with Lieutenant Dudington interfering, so a man named Joseph Bucklin shot him with a musket ball. This was to be the first British casualty by firearm in the American Revolution. On June 10, having shot the commander and captured the crew, the Rhode Islanders set fire to the ship. King George offered a hefty reward for the names of any guilty parties, but a plague of spot amnesia seemed to come over all Rhode Island.

Gaspee amnesia seems to still leave people forgetting this momentous event, but the Gaspee Days Committee was formed in 1965 to make sure that folks remember. There was a great bicentennial *Gaspee*-burning celebration in 1972, and Gaspee Days are now celebrated each June to commemorate the real start of the Revolution. With colonial costumes, food, and even a reenactment of the boat-burning itself, Gaspee Days are much more fun than some tea party. Visit www.gaspee.com or call (401) 781–1772 if you have a burning desire for more details.

> *Boston's Tea Party fame should be less,*
> *Since Rhode Islanders had such success*
> *That they captured the crew*
> *And then burned the ship too!*
> *That's the value of having good press.*

On Thin Ice
Warwick

John Langella plays hockey. And as a hockey player, he needs to attend each match with the proper equipment: puck, stick, snorkel.

Snorkel? Yes, snorkel. Underwater hockey may not be a very well-known sport at the moment, but John Langella is helping to change

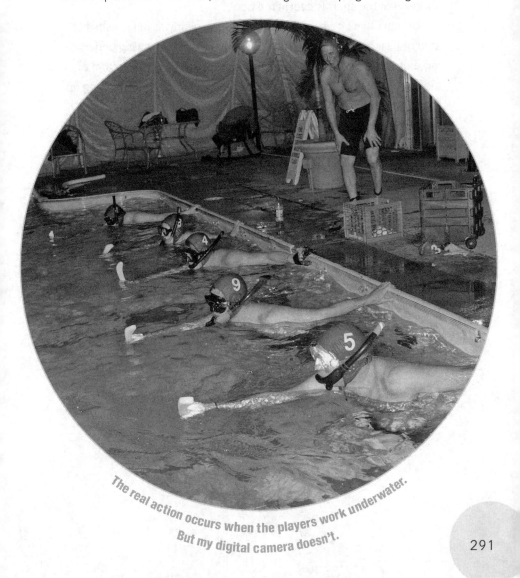

The real action occurs when the players work underwater. But my digital camera doesn't.

that. John was a free diver and spear fisher for many years, so he has a natural affinity for the water. Underwater hockey is much bigger in England, but few people in the States have heard of it, and most of them live in California. That's why John brought it to Rhode Island. He got some of his friends from the diving community to join, and convinced a bunch of former hockey players whose knees couldn't withstand ice hockey that the sport is cool in the pool.

But don't think it's easy. Sure, there aren't nearly as many fistfights as in regular hockey (even if there were, it'd be hard to swing underwater), but the sport is exhausting. All the play occurs on the bottom of the pool while holding your breath, with players constantly popping up for air. It's a team sport, but often feels individual when it comes to holding your breath, not to mention needing to worry about three dimensions instead of two.

Naturally, when John tells people about underwater hockey, they don't believe him. But after going online to see if it's real, they come to watch. Unfortunately, you can't really see much unless you're underwater, so the spectators end up jumping in. As John describes it, they say, "What a bunch of crazy people . . . let me try that!"

They generally play at Healththrax Fitness & Wellness in Warwick, with everyone chipping in to pay for renting the pool. So show up on a Thursday night, or e-mail John at biodiver@cox.net. For him, the best part of the sport is the camaraderie of playing an intense small sport, so he'd love to hear from you. In fact, drop him an e-mail, and your first time will be free. After all, given global warming, underwater hockey may just be the wave of the future.

INDEX

INDEX

INDEX

INDEX

INDEX

INDEX

INDEX

About the Author

Seth Brown has been writing
professionally for more than a
decade, and boy is his wrist
tired. In 1997 he began a
weekly rhyming political humor
column for the *Providence Journal.* His writing has appeared in
various publications ranging from
the *Patriot Ledger* to *USA Today.* His
first book, *Think You're the Only One?:*
Oddball Groups Where Outsiders Fit In, was

published by Barnes & Noble in 2004. His column, "The Pun Also Rises,"
appears in the *North Adams Transcript* on Fridays and won second
place in the New England Press Association's 2006 awards for humor
columnists.

   Born in East Greenwich, Seth didn't spend much time outside of
Rhode Island until college. He graduated from Williams College, where
he founded a humor magazine (which still exists) and a classical kazoo
quintet (which does not). Seth produces the *Leth & Sex Podcast* along
with Lex Friedman. He contributes short jokes to the *Washington Post*'s
Style Invitational, limericks to BBSpot.com, and very little to society.

   Seth's Web site is www.RisingPun.com.